Woman
to
Woman

Woman to Woman

Preparing Yourself to Mentor

Edna Ellison and Tricia Scribner

new
hope
PUBLISHERS

Birmingham, Alabama

New Hope® Publishers
P. O. Box 12065
Birmingham, AL 35202-2065
www.newhopepublishers.com

Library of Congress Cataloging-in-Publication Data
Ellison, Edna.
Woman to woman : preparing yourself to mentor / Edna Ellison and Tricia Scribner.
p. cm.
Originally published: c1999.
ISBN 1-56309-949-7 (pbk.)
1. Church work with women. 2. Interpersonal relations-Religious aspects-Christianity. 3. Female friendship-Religious aspects-Christianity. 4. Mentoring in church work. I. Scribner, Tricia. II. Title.
BV4445.E45 2005
253'.082--dc22
2005008105

ISBN: 1-56309-949-7

N054121 • 0805 • 5M1

TABLE OF CONTENTS

PREFACE

(left) Tricia Scribner, R.M., M.S.N.
(right) Edna Ellison, Ph.D.

Woman to Woman: Preparing Yourself to Mentor is actually a detour Tricia Scribner and I took from writing a larger book on mentoring. Several years ago while Tricia and I lived in the same city in California, we embarked on an exciting mentoring relationship in Christian writing. At that time, mentoring was rapidly becoming a hot topic among people in the Christian community, as well as the business world. Based on our own experience in a mentoring relationship, we began surveying women in eleven states and three countries about their mentoring experiences and feelings about the process.

Our findings described first person what we had learned already from current literature. Today's mobile Baby Boomers are the first generation of Americans who often live far from extended family—those who provided in-house mentoring experiences for the previous generation of women. Though not able to define the void in their lives concisely, today's women often flounder in life experiences without the support and encouragement of more mature women who have already traveled the road and weathered the storms successfully.

Women in the survey who had been mentored clearly valued the connection the relationship provided, as well as the truths they learned. Based on our research, Tricia and I began writing a book that addressed many aspects of the mentoring phenomenon in this country today, while focusing on the specific needs of Christian women.

After I moved to Mississippi, Tricia came to Jackson for several days to work on the book. We discussed the recurring concern voiced by Christian women's leaders that they needed an interactive Bible study to prepare the mentor for the mentoring experience. Many women, they said, when approached about mentoring someone, expressed apprehension, a foggy view of what the role would involve, and concern that they had nothing to offer. After talking and praying about the need for about 24 hours, Tricia and I laid aside the larger book and detoured into the subject area of preparing mentors to mentor. This book is the joyous result.

We are blessed to have the opportunity to co-write a book that we believe is God's gift to affirm, encourage, and exhort you, the mentor, to be who you really are: His chosen, holy vessel.

—Edna Ellison

The word *mentor* has been around a long time. We had no dilemma deciding what to call the helper in the mentoring relationship, but what could we call the one being mentored? Writers have already coined words to define this person. *Mentoree* and *mentee* were the two most often used words we found in our search (we also found *apprentice*, *protégé*, and, in a more structured setting, *client*.) However, *mentoree* and *mentee* are simply derivations of the word *mentor*, and the person being mentored is so much more than an extension of the mentor.

So what could we call her? Could we coin a new word that would more closely reflect how the Lord, our Mentor, sees us, His followers and loved ones?

The question took me on a search for words used in the Bible in the original Hebrew and Greek. The word not only had to define accurately the role of being mentored, but also had to have a nice ring to it. It needed to sound lovely and gentle—a word you could hug!

I found several good words: regel in the Old Testament meant "follow" or "at thy feet." Great meaning, but not soft enough. In the New Testament, the word mimetes meant "a follower or imitator." Problem is, it was difficult to pronounce. Not a word we could easily use.

Then I read the story of Ruth, a poignant picture of the mentoring relationship between two women. Naomi guided Ruth through some very delicate situations as Ruth pursued a husband and provider. And Ruth, well, she was a jewel of a lady. How many women do you know who convert to their mother-in-law's religion and promise to stay by her side "till death do us part" (Ruth 1:17)?

Clearly, their bond went deeper than the average mother-in-law and daughter-in-law relationship. They functioned in more than teacher/learner roles as well. They were dear friends: interdependent. They needed each other. Naomi needed Ruth with her youthfulness and hope for building a future on which they both would survive since both their husbands had died. During that time, women didn't complain that men climbed the corporate ladder faster. There was no corporate ladder for women to climb. When a husband died, the wife had little hope of survival without family assistance. Ruth, on the other hand, needed Naomi's wisdom and advice and eagerly asked for it.

Seeing Ruth as the one being mentored, I looked up her name and should not have been surprised to learn that Ruth means "friend." Considering the mentoree as a friend was appropriate, but since the word *friend* has been trivialized in our society, I wasn't sure it was strong enough.

I wondered what word Jesus, the Mentor, used for His mentorees, the disciples? I found the answer in John 15:15: "No longer do I call you slaves, for the slave does not know what his master is doing; but I have called you friends, for all things that I have heard from my Father I have made known to you" (NASB). Jesus called His mentorees His "friends," and as friends He shared with them all He learned from the Father!

I wondered if there was a beautiful, huggable word for our word *friend* in the Hebrew or Greek languages of the Bible. My search ended when I found the word for friend in the Old Testament: merea (pronounced "may-RAY-ah," or as we have Americanized it, "mah-RAY-ah"). Any way you say it, it's beautiful—merea. Say it aloud a few times and listen to its gentle sound. Now that's a word you can hug!

My search complete, I thanked the Lord for such a gorgeous word, a word He coined for Ruth and Naomi's time, long before He came to earth and on one certain day honored His mentorees by calling them friends.

John 15:13 says, "Greater love has no one than this, that one lay down his life for his friends" (NASB). Most of us will not be called upon to lay down our lives in death for the cause of Christ. But when you reach out to a woman who is spiritually younger, pull her up beside you, wrap your arms around her shoulders, and walk with her, you have laid down your life for your dear friend: your merea. You may call her a disciple, a mentee, or a follower, but first call her your "merea."

—Tricia Scribner

ACKNOWLEDGMENTS

From Edna

Sincere thanks to my dear family: my son, Jack, who has always supported me and encouraged me; and his wife, Wendy, my favorite daughter-in-law, who has given me technical advice on computer snarls as I tried to transfer the manuscript to the wonderful New Hope editorial team: Jennifer Law, Amy Montgomery, and Leslie Caldwell.

I also owe thanks to my daughter, Patsy, who has taught me much about mentoring. She is a model merea, and we have an ideal mother-daughter mentoring relationship. Her husband, Tim, my favorite son-in-law, has encouraged us through illness and tragedy as we wrote this book.

This effort would not have been completed without the hundreds of women in the United States and Europe who responded to our survey, which became the basis for our research on mentoring. Many of them shared personal stories of their lives. Thanks also go to state women's leaders who shared, collected, and returned surveys to us for the book.

From Tricia

Thank you, Randy, my husband, for navigating me through the netherworld of long distance intercomputer communication (meaning, "Edna, why didn't you get that chapter I emailed?"). Neli, Sara, and Emily, my children, I appreciate the sacrifices you made as I wrote this book.

Daddy, thanks for instilling in me a love for writing. Mama, your quiet strength is ever undergirding me. Sis, thanks for reading the manuscript and laughing at just the right moments.

Dear women mentors of Woodward Park Baptist, may the Lord bless you for volunteering to be the first group of women mentors to complete this study, for giving me feedback, and for committing to being mentor learners.

Renaee Deck, Trish Hester, Teresa Watts, Jennifer McInnes, Ronda Huffman, Jim Edmiston, and Jackie Wojdylak, thanks for being friends who encouraged me and for never saying, "You look awfully tired for a person who doesn't have a real job." Daisy Hepburn of Scottsdale Bible Church, what a jump start your support gave us!

Dear Lord Jesus, I hope the women who read this book see your smile. Thanks for giving me a life work that fills me with so much joy it spills over onto paper.

Edna, writing is hard work. Even so, I've loved every minute of writing this book with you (except when I lost the manuscript trying to transfer from a backup disk). Thanks for being my mentor, but most of all for being my friend.

INTRODUCTION

As a Christian mentor, you are about to embark on one of the most rewarding adventures for a child of God. We hope you will find this book helpful as you prepare for the journey alongside your merea. (The word *merea* will be used throughout this Bible study to denote the one being mentored.) We have written about women's experiences because the respondents to our survey were women, but men will find this book helpful as they prepare to mentor someone.

The following pages contain 18 interactive studies. You may complete one study per day, five days a week, and you will complete the book in about a month. Another option is to complete one study per week along with other mentors, meeting together each week for discussion and support, finishing in about four months. Working through the studies over a longer period of time allows you to process and apply the concepts more fully. A group study guide is provided in the back of this book for guiding discussion. You may wish to combine studies and complete the course in twelve weeks.

You may choose to complete this book before entering the mentoring relationship, or you may complete it after beginning your relationship with your merea. However you use this book, our prayer is that these studies will affirm and challenge you.

Pause at each item and carefully work through the interactive questions. After you have completed each question, you will find below it some suggested responses. Remember, there are seldom right or wrong answers in an interactive Bible study. The purpose is that you think about your life and search your heart as God leads you.

Feel free to process your thoughts or even write your responses in the margins on each page. And if the Lord takes you in a new direction, a detour from the words and blanks written on the page, go with Him!

At the end of each day's study is a pithy saying to encourage you and sometimes make you chuckle. We labeled it ARNF, which stands for Always Remember and Never Forget. The ARNF is spelled out in the first chapter, but abbreviated each chapter thereafter.

The two of us collaborated on every page of this book. However, for the sake of clarity, especially of the personal illustrations you read, we have designated the primary writer of each segment.

At the end of this book is a resource section which contains:

- a brief study guide for a facilitator of mentors who choose to meet once a week in a small group to share their feelings about what they've learned;
- a sample covenant for you and your merea to use;
- a commissioning service, to be used in your church to consecrate mentors for service;
- a reference list of books or resources you may read for a deeper study of issues related to mentoring and self-growth;
- a list of fun things to do with your merea; and
- a guide for how this book can be used in churchwide settings.

May God bless you as you embark on the mentoring adventure and become a part of the Merea Movement that is changing the lives of women for Christ!

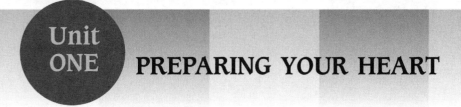

CHAPTER ONE
Do I Have the Stuff Mentors Are Made Of?

The word mentor may conjure up a variety of images for you. A wide range of definitions of mentoring saturate the secular and the Christian world.

Check the definition which most closely describes how you view mentoring.

❑ "Mentoring . . . means using the best part of yourself to help another see and become the best that they can be."
> —Esther Burroughs, Coral Gables, Florida

❑ "Mentoring occurs when a woman who is older and wiser, with experience, takes a younger woman under her wing to share, teach, and train her."
> —Lynette McElroy, Sidney, Nebraska

❑ "One with wisdom, knowledge and experience greater than the one with whom the wisdom is shared, who guides, accepts, and holds accountable another."
> —Lynna Rea Sargent, Springhill, Louisiana

❑ "A mentor is a trusted counselor, guide, tutor, or coach."
> —Donna Otto, Scottsdale, Arizona

❑ "Someone who shares God-given wisdom with someone else on a regular basis with the aim of encouraging that person in bite-sized bits to live a life that is pleasing to God."
> —Paula Scantlebury, Farfields-Sunnyside, England

In your own words, write your definition of a mentor.

_____

_____

_____

ME, A MENTOR?

Do you approach the prospect of mentoring with mixed feelings? Most of us do. Circle the following feelings you have experienced about mentoring.

joy	confidence	apprehension	uncertainty
confusion	awe	inadequacy	fear
eagerness	lack of focus	anxiety	peace

What reasons cause women to avoid serving as mentors? In talking with many women, we have discovered some common concerns. Check those which express your feelings.

- ❏ I don't want to appear prideful.
- ❏ I don't have anything to offer.
- ❏ I might not know the answers to her questions.
- ❏ I just don't have the time.
- ❏ I don't know enough about the Bible.
- ❏ I feel inadequate for the task.
- ❏ I don't know what a mentor does.

COMPETING WITH THE TITUS 2 WOMAN

One reason women feel inadequate to mentor is that they compare themselves with an imaginary, heroic, Christian woman who leaps tall buildings in a single bound and also teaches a women's Bible study.

Titus 2:3 is probably the Scripture most often used as a guideline for mentoring. **Read Titus 2:3. How do you feel after reading this passage?**

_____

_____

_____

_____

If you said, "Whew! What a job description, and where's the back door?" join the ranks. The requirements of Titus 2:3 can be rather intimidating.

I have a bone to pick with the writer of this verse. First, I don't like being called an "older woman." Despite my wrinkles and flapping underarms, I'm a mere babe compared to my friend, Miss Ludie, now 96 years old. Second, the phrase "reverent in behavior" (NASB) sounds like I'll never again be able to tuck my nightshirt in my shorts and go out in the yard to prune roses. Third, I have never gossiped maliciously, only with the best intent. Fourth, I'm definitely not enslaved to wine. (However, I have been known to down a full jar of marshmallow cream in less than two minutes when overcome by a sugar craving.) Last, I'd be glad to teach what is good. Just give me the outline of what that includes and a mild sedative 30 minutes before I speak. And could you give me a podium that's high enough for me to rest my chin if I feel faint?

Many times I don't feel qualified to mentor. The problem is that by the time I do feel qualified I'll be in heaven with the Lord. While that's great for me, it doesn't do much for Mary Smith down here on earth looking for someone to help her grow.

QUALIFIED AND CALLED

When 189 Christian women in Virginia were surveyed regarding what they wanted in leaders, the top four prized characteristics were:

1. commitment;
2. love and trust of God, Christ, and others;
3. dedication to God and the church;
4. compassion and caring.

As you reflect on these characteristics, consider what qualifies you to serve as a mentor. **Read the following and check the ones which apply to you.**

❑ I have committed my life to Jesus Christ.

❑ I love the Savior and seek to obey Him.

❑ Christ has walked with me through difficult life experiences.

❑ At times I have hurt, failed, fallen, and floundered.

❑ I have endured disappointment.

❑ I feel compassion for the plight of another.

❑ I am growing in my understanding of God's trustworthiness.

❑ I sense that God wants me to serve as a mentor.

How many did you check? You are more qualified than you think. Qualification does not come with educational degrees, age (necessarily), or other accomplishments. Instead, you are qualified in your heart. Christ qualifies you because you are a witness to His presence and love within your life experiences.

Serving as a mentor doesn't imply that you are fully mature. In fact, you may have a mentor while you mentor someone else. Serving as an effective mentor does mean that you are open to Christ, learning and growing, and actively pursuing your own wholeness (maturity). The greatest gift you can give your merea is yourself, given out of your fullness in Christ, not out of obligation or needing to prove something.

So while you pursue the godly characteristics of Titus 2:3, remember that even Paul did not view himself as having reached the pinnacle of righteousness, but continually reached forward in obedience (Phil. 3:12).

FROM RESISTANCE TO RESOLVE

A few years ago, we had a very large Irish Setter dog we called Elijah. (I wonder if the prophet would be honored or offended?) Since he was a house dog, we bathed him in our big bathtub—at least we tried. As soon as he heard water running and spied me walking toward him, his eyes bulged, his ears drooped, and he tried to hide his 65-pound frame under any object more than 6 inches off the floor. Once he was caught, we'd have to carry him because pulling him was like trying to move a bulldozer. Getting him through the bathroom door was no picnic either. He writhed, flailed, and clawed; you'd think he was going to the gas chamber.

If you are experiencing that kind of resistance about mentoring, then slow down, take a breath, and give yourself permission to take the time you need to make a wise decision. But know that some feelings of apprehension are completely normal, even once you are involved in the mentoring process.

Moses experienced apprehension when God called him to lead the Israelites out of Egypt to freedom. But God was not dependent upon Moses' ability to accomplish the task. He wanted Moses to depend on Him instead of his own ability.

Read Exodus 3:7–10 and 4:10–12. Now read an adapted version of what God said to His servant, Moses, and is saying to you as well. In the blanks, write Moses' fearful response in your own words.

v. 7: I have seen your merea's troubles. I have heard her cry. I am concerned about her pain, and I have come to help her through you. I will bring her out of that land and lead her into a good land, a fertile land. So now I am sending you.

v. 11: **But Lord,** _____

_____

_____

_____

_____

v. 12: *I will be with you. This will be proof that I am sending you. After you lead her out, you both will worship me in this place.*

v. 4–10: *But Lord,* _____

_____

_____

_____

    v. 11: *Who made your mouth? It is I, the LORD. Now go. I will help you speak, and I will teach you what to say.*

Pray: "Even so, Lord, send me."

    As you enter the mentoring relationship, know that God is walking with you.
Read 1 Thessalonians 5:24 (NASB):

    "Faithful is He who calls you, and he also will bring it to pass."

Affirm your trust in God as you fill in the blanks below.

_____ is He who _____ you, and He also will _____ it to _____.

━━━━━ **Always Remember, Never Forget** ━━━━━

Don't wait until you are perfect to mentor. By then all your teeth will have fallen out and no one will be able to understand you.

CHAPTER TWO
Me, Gifted?

As we discussed in the first study, Christian women have many reasons preventing them from mentoring. Many women feel that they don't have anything to offer. The truth is "God don't make no junk."

America's educational system provides specialized classes for the small percentage of children who excel in certain subject areas. In God's educational system the gifted classes are completely full because every single Christian is endowed with gifts. So if you are feeling unworthy or unable, sit back and soak up the truth of this chapter. The Lord wishes to show you a mirror of what He sees in you!

Read Ephesians 4:11–16. What is God's purpose in gifting each of His children?

_____

_____

_____

God intends that we each use our unique gifts (talents, skills, and spiritual gifts) to strengthen and mature one another.

UNIQUELY GIFTED

God has gifted you in three major ways. You have natural gifts which are often called talents. You also have developed skills through training which are learned gifts. In addition, when you gave your life to Jesus Christ, the Lord's Spirit gave you spiritual gifts to use for building up the church body. While natural gifts, learned gifts, and spiritual gifts may overlap, each offers unique qualities to your repertoire of giftedness.

1. Natural Gifts

Natural gifts are often called talents. A talent is an area of ability in which you naturally feel comfortable and excel—it comes easily to you. Some of your talents may have been identified even in childhood. Neli, my oldest daughter, is gifted artistically. She has doodled on everything in sight since she was quite young.

While you may improve your skill in a talent through practice, chances are you possess an innate knack for it. Talents may include such abilities as playing the piano, mechanical ability, having a green thumb with plants, or having a way of making others feel comfortable. Sometimes talents are easier to describe than name.

Read Acts 9:1–2. Identify Paul's natural gifts, apparent even before he became a Christian.

_____

_____

Paul's determination, zeal, and verbal persuasive abilities are evident in these verses. God gifted Paul with natural talents, and Paul would use them for God's glory after his conversion.

Read Acts 26:24–29. How did God use Paul's natural zeal, determination, and persuasive abilities to spread the gospel?

_____

_____

_____

_____

List or describe some of your talents.

_____

_____

_____

2. Learned Gifts

Skills are tasks in which you demonstrate learned proficiency. That is, you're good at a task because you invested the effort to learn, practice, and master it. Skills may be learned at school or at home. If your mom taught you how to make bread, that's a skill—a skill many women of the boomer generation have not mastered (but would like to). Like talents, sometimes skills are easier to describe than name.

Our friend, Jorge, helps make our yard look beautiful. Jorge knows how much water is enough, but not too much. He can tell me which plants will bloom next year and which ones won't. He checks our sprinkler system and cuts back our palm trees. Jorge spent years learning and even apprenticed under someone to master the skill. I find it difficult to label what he does as gardening because he knows and does so much more. But I can describe his skill and my yard shows his giftedness.

Some skills require formal training. Diane Varady of Hayward, California, uses the principles of Christian Women's Job Corps. She mentors women in computer literacy to help them move toward self-reliance in the work world. She worked very hard to learn computer skills well enough to teach others.

Read Acts 18:1–3. Identify one of Paul's skills. _____

Describe or name skills you have developed over the years.

_____

_____

_____

_____

_____

3. Spiritual Gifts

Spiritual gifts are given to a new believer by the Holy Spirit for the purpose of helping other Christians grow and strengthening the church in general. All spiritual gifts ultimately are expressed for glorifying Christ (to make Him shine before others). You need not worry about becoming prideful as you seek to identify and share your spiritual gifts. They are given by the Spirit—you did nothing to earn them or deserve them. You, as a Christian, possess at least one (1 Cor. 12:7, 11) because you are God's honored child, and His plan for you is that from the moment of your new birth your actions make eternal impact for His kingdom.

Many women we surveyed described what they felt they had to offer a merea in terms of spiritual giftedness. Encouragement, service, teaching, wisdom (application), and sharing Bible knowledge are examples of spiritual gifts that women have found helpful in a mentoring ministry. **Review the following Scriptures which describe spiritual gifts. List below the spiritual gifts you identify in each passage.**

Romans 12:6–8

_____

_____

_____

1 Corinthians 12:8–10, 28–30

_____

_____

_____

Ephesians 4:11

_____

_____

_____

1 Peter 4:9–11

_____

_____

_____

How many did you find? **Compare your list with our master list below.**

We identified each gift only once since some gifts are identified in several places. Remember that this list is not comprehensive. Other gifts are mentioned throughout the Bible.

- Prophesying
- Serving
- Teaching
- Encouraging
- Giving
- Leadership
- Mercy
- Wisdom
- Knowledge
- Hospitality

- Faith
- Healing
- Miracles
- Discernment
- Speaking in tongues
- Interpretation of tongues
- Apostleship
- Evangelism
- Pastoring

Read Acts 19:8. What spiritual gift do you see in Paul in this Scripture?

_____

_____

_____

Paul was gifted as an evangelist who preached the truth. Many people believed in Christ because he used his gift to serve the Lord.

Describe your spiritual gift(s).

_____

_____

If you want to better understand the meaning and use of gifts or if you wish to identify areas of your own spiritual giftedness, invest yourself in learning more. As you prayerfully consider the possibilities, study books on spiritual giftedness such as Yours for the Giving: Spiritual Gifts by Barbara Joiner and Uniquely Gifted by Stuart Calvert. As you study, ask friends what gifts they see in you. Ask yourself what areas of service bring you joy. Ask the Lord to reveal how He has uniquely gifted you.

TALENT, SKILL, OR SPIRITUAL GIFT?

You may have difficulty deciding whether your gift is natural, learned, or spiritual. Sometimes a gift seems to belong in all three categories. For instance, I sing in a choir, with a small group, and as a soloist.

I began singing in public as a young child. Because I enjoyed it, I developed this natural gift through years of practice and study with voice and piano teachers to improve my skill. I committed my life to Christ as a young child, and the Lord has used my voice to show His mercy, to encourage, and to heal others emotionally. For me singing is a natural talent, a learned gift, and a spiritual gift. More important than placing a gift in the proper category is knowing that God has gifted you because He loves you and wants to express His love to another through you.

UNIQUELY YOU

One point to remember: a spiritual gift will be expressed uniquely through your personality. A dear friend, Aline, was a home economist who served as a missionary, opening her home to hundreds of guests. Aline made cakes only from scratch, never from a mix, and rarely opened a can since all her veggies were prepared fresh. One look at her, and I quickly crossed the gift of hospitality (1 Peter 4:9–10) off my list of possible spiritual gifts. I got hives just thinking about baking a cake without Betty Crocker.

Years later a group of women sat around my kitchen table munching snacks and planning a project. As we chatted about dates and deadlines, one of the ladies stopped and said, "Tricia, you have such a gift of hospitality."

I could feel the tears threatening. Me? The gift of hospitality? "You should meet my friend, Aline," I said.

She said, "Tricia, you open your home and make us feel comfortable."

It came to me that hospitality was not about cakes but about the openness of the heart. While Aline has the gift of hospitality, so do I!

Your natural, learned, and spiritual gifts are tremendous internal resources which you bring to a mentoring relationship. You have identified some of your areas of giftedness. Continue to think of more and add them to your lists over the coming days.

GIFTED ENOUGH

Once you acknowledge your giftedness, you may doubt your ability to mentor because of what you see yourself lacking. You may think, "I'm comfortable inviting her over for coffee, but if she asks me a question about the Bible, I'll faint."

Read 1 Corinthians 12:14–20. Write in one sentence what you believe to be the main point of this passage:

_____

_____

_____

None of us individually possesses all spiritual gifts (or natural or learned gifts, for that matter). That's why we need each other. Use your resources when you hit a tough spot or an unfamiliar area. Be honest about areas in which you need help or guidance. Then, thank the Lord for making you uniquely you and bless your merea's life with your giftedness!

———— Always Remember, Never Forget ————

Cake mix or no cake mix, you're gifted!

CHAPTER THREE
What's in It for Me?

Megan was the first one to volunteer for our mentoring program at church. She wrote her name in the "Mentors" column of the sign-up sheet while the ink was still hot from the office printer. Filled with enthusiasm, she couldn't wait to begin.

Throughout our training, the mentors' prayer retreat, and the opening tea, Megan made the program a priority, canceling family outings to attend every mentors' session.

On the day we introduced mentors to their mereas, she sat on the front row of our chapel, beaming as she was paired with Anne, an attractive young blond. Only two weeks later I saw Anne at church, wiping her eyes, hurriedly leaving our women's coordinator's office.

"What's up?" I asked Vaughn, our coordinator.

"I was afraid of this," Vaughn said. "Megan just told Anne to find another mentor. She's quitting."

"What made you afraid Megan would give up?"

Vaughn hesitated. "I don't want to say anything unkind. Let's just say Megan is . . . needy."

"Aren't we all!"

"Yes, in some ways. I mean, I believe Megan is spiritually, maybe emotionally needy. Sometimes I question her motives."

Within a week, Vaughn called and asked me to mentor Anne. I agreed, but felt a little apprehensive because the previous relationship had gone sour. It was so important that this new relationship succeed for Anne; I did not want her to be hurt again. I remembered what Vaughn had said about motives the day Anne left her office in tears. I began to question my own motives. Was I mentoring, as Megan did, because I needed to be needed? Did I really want to help Anne, or did I want to make myself look good before other church women and gain a young friend who would admire me?

At our first meeting, I gave Anne the opportunity to talk about her experience with Megan. I asked what could have made the mentoring experience better for her, hoping to find what went wrong so I could avoid the same situation. Anne explained:

"When I first met Megan in our fellowship hall, she smiled at me, but her eyes were looking around at other women. When she bear hugged me the first day, I felt ill at ease because I hardly knew her. Plus, I wanted to sit in the back of the room, but she dragged me down front! I was so uncomfortable!

"At the tea she moved me from leader to leader—Vaughn, Mrs. Dean, Dr. Dorothy —gushing and saying she was showing me off. I just wanted a friend, a spiritual leader, not a social climber.

"At our next meeting, at her house, she spent 45 minutes showing me her antique furniture and porcelain doll collection. I was short of time that day. I went home feeling cheated. I called her several times that week, but she never returned my calls. Then on Thursday, I had a real crisis at home. My husband, Tim, threatened to leave me. I called Megan for support. She seemed preoccupied as we talked, but she interrupted me twice to say, 'Men are all alike, the morons!'

"I asked if she had ever experienced this kind of conflict with her husband. She became angry and told me never to ask her that question again. I cried myself to sleep that night. I flipped through the pages of my Bible, trying to find Scripture to comfort me, but nothing helped. If only Megan had given me one good verse to hang on to.

"The next day I found she had told the biggest gossip in town about my trouble with Tim. I guess I'm disillusioned with mentors, but I know that I need one. I hope I'm realistic in believing I can find one who cares and who takes my problems seriously."

TAKING A HARD LOOK AT MOTIVES
How do you feel after reading about Anne's experience?

_____

_____

_____

List below Megan's behaviors that indicate impure motives.

_____

_____

_____

If Megan had honestly discerned her own motives, perhaps she would have realized that she should address her own neediness before taking on the demands of serving as a mentor. Her neediness did not disqualify her from ever serving as mentor, but it did signal a warning that the time was not right for her to serve in the role.

AVOIDING THE PITFALLS

You can avoid the pitfalls that entrapped Megan by asking yourself hard questions before you embrace the responsibilities of mentoring.

Read the following paragraphs, responding to the questions in each section.

A. Am I performing?

Have you ever shaken hands with someone who smiled and then looked past you to a more important person? How did you feel? Megan's first mistake was to smile at her merea while looking at others. Respect your merea by giving her your attention and care.

Megan also showed false affection for Anne. She hugged her too warmly, too soon. Remember that some people don't ever want to be hugged; a simple handshake the first time you meet will suffice.

At the mentors' introduction session, Megan operated in a keep-your-eyes-on-me mode. Dragging Anne to the front row demonstrated insensitivity to Anne's feelings. Moving from leader to leader, showing Anne off, indicated her true motive: impressing those she considered higher on the godliness scale.

Read Matthew 6:1–6 and answer the following questions.

• **Substitute women for the word men in verse 1. Why is it a serious matter if you are mentoring just to impress other women so they'll think you are a godly model for others?**

_____

_____

• **In verses 2–6, do you think Jesus' warning not to brag about your giving pertains only to giving money? If not, how does it apply to you as a mentor?**

_____

_____

Remember the firm warning in verse 1 that "you will have no reward from your Father in heaven" if you act righteously to be seen by others. Schedule a time with a trusted friend this week to discuss any pressure you feel to perform.

B. Am I self-absorbed?

As you listed Megan's insensitive behaviors, you may have noted her showing Anne her antiques and dolls rather than listening to Anne's need. Often we remain absorbed in the physical realm, concerned with ourselves and our things, when we need to explore the emotional world of our merea's feelings and lead her to the spiritual realm of God's healing.

_____

_____

_____

What do you think Megan's motive was when she spent 45 minutes showing Anne her antiques and dolls on a day Anne had so little time?

_____

_____

_____

List things or activities which absorb your attention and may hinder your ability to focus on your merea's needs.

_____

_____

_____

C. Am I out to lunch?

Megan never returned Anne's calls. If your motive is sincerely helping your merea, you will not ignore her.

Megan was not a good listener. She seemed preoccupied, Anne said. She was "out to lunch" during a crisis. Megan may have proclaimed her eagerness to mentor, but her heart wasn't in it.

Recall a time when you were not a good listener. What was the result?

_____

_____

_____

Describe actions that will demonstrate to your merea that you are interested in what she has to say.

_____

_____

_____

D. Am I angry or defensive?

When Megan interrupted Anne, she showed rudeness, impatience, and lack of respect. She was also defensive about her own husband, becoming openly angry with Anne.

Ask yourself the following questions:

1. **Does anger or frustration in any area of my life paralyze me?**

2. **Am I expecting my merea to serve as a convenient sounding board for my own frustrations?**

3. **Am I too stressed out or emotionally empty to mentor someone?**

If you answered "yes" to any of the above questions, talk with a trusted friend about how you can first meet your own needs before embarking on a mentoring relationship.

E. Do I need to be needed?

Sometimes people volunteer to mentor because they need to be needed. With their nurturing tendencies, women are especially vulnerable to this entrapment. Be sure you are not mentoring to gain satisfaction and praise from an adoring merea who desperately needs you.

Imagine your merea disagreeing with you on the meaning of a Scripture passage or how to apply a truth in her life.

How do you feel in that situation?

_____

_____

In disagreeing with you, your merea implies she doesn't need your opinion. If that imaginary scene caused you significant anxiety, talk with someone about your expectations of the mentoring relationship.

F. Can I keep a confidence?

Finally, Megan committed the cardinal sin for mentors: betraying a confidence. What a merea expresses within the mentoring relationship is not to be shared elsewhere—not with other mentors, not with your prayer partner, not even with your best friend. (We will discuss this further in a later study.)

Ask yourself the following questions:

1. Do I enjoy being the first person to tell explosive news?

2. Am I happy when I know everything that is going on and disappointed when I'm left out of the circle of information?

PRAYING ABOUT YOUR MOTIVES

Can you think of any way you show pride in your own ability, rather than acknowledging God's authority in the mentoring relationship?

_____

_____

_____

_____

Read Psalm 139:23–24. Ask God to make you alert to offensive or hurtful motives. Write below what God shows you:

_____

_____

_____

_____

Taking the time to evaluate honestly your reasons for mentoring can be difficult. But discerning your motives before entering a mentoring relationship dramatically enhances your chance for success.

———— Always Remember, Never Forget ————

"What's in it for Me?" is a fair question, but if it's the only question, you're not ready to mentor.

CHAPTER FOUR
Where Do I Grow from Here?

When it comes to spiritual maturity I feel like the lady, who, after several failed attempts at finding the road to a nearby town, stopped at a country gas station and asked the attendant for directions.

His response was (after spitting on the ground, of course), "Ya' can't get there from here." Sometimes maturity seems that far out of reach.

I've always been glad that I became a Christian as a young child. But the older I get, the more embarrassed I've become that I haven't grown more, read more Scripture, and saved more of the world. I still battle jealousy, insecurity, and depression. Some days I'm irritable, demanding, and selfish–and those aren't even my PMS days!

When I'm forced to confront my glaring weaknesses, I usually respond like Edna who complained to me about her bargain knee–high hose. "I bought three packages of these hose because they were on sale for 50 cents each. I've only worn them once and the band at the top is already sprung out."

She pulled up her pants leg and sure enough, the hose sagged like an accordion around her ankle. Instead of removing the hose and facing the humiliation of a bare ankle, she said, "I think I'll just pull my pants leg down a little bit and no one will notice."

Like Edna, I too prefer to pull my pants legs down a little bit to hide those things in my life the Lord desires to peel and heal. I'm not alone in my struggle with weakness. Christian psychotherapist Larry Crabb said, "I've had to admit that I still struggle with a lot of the same problems people pay me to help them deal with . . . I thought I'd be farther along the path toward maturity...." Finally, a comrade in the foxhole!

During this study, take an honest look at your spiritual life. Set aside extra time to complete the two self-evaluation tools. Rather than rushing through them, complete them at two different times if needed.

SELF-EVALUATION OR SPIRIT ILLUMINATION

I dread the self-evaluations we complete in Bible study class. The ranking options usually range from, 1 = "I do this holy thing even in my sleep" to 5 =

"I'm slime." I fear marking "5" will reveal what I fear most, that in the deepest part of me I am really bad. I avoid marking "1" thinking God might teach me a life-lesson on pride. Generally, I mark a lot of safe, middle-of-the-road 3s, and stuff the survey in my Bible where no one can see it.

But isn't self-evaluation necessary? Doesn't the growing Christian take a look at the heart now and then to see how things are going? The truth is, more than self-evaluation we need Holy Spirit illumination. As He peels away the external shell, His light of truth shines on the dark places we've hidden, cleansing and healing us.

ALL GROWN UP AND NO PLACE TO GO?

Our first survey will help you discern whether you are spiritually grown up enough to mentor. Please do not base your decision whether to mentor on the results of this questionnaire alone. We will provide several tools to help you evaluate various aspects of readiness, and you will also want to consider other variables in your decision.

READY OR NOT SURVEY
Check the box beside each statement which describes you.

I would describe myself as:

- ❏ 1. A good person, but I do not have a personal relationship with Jesus.
- ❏ 2. Not a good person, but I do have a personal relationship with Jesus.
- ❏ 3. Experienced in many areas of life (including being a Christian for years) and feel capable of giving support to others.
- ❏ 4. Not experienced, but I have just become a Christian and want to grow in my faith.
- ❏ 5. Spiritually mature, but I'm not sure I could guide anyone else.
- ❏ 6. Not a perfect person, but I have been through the fire and found God able to take me through the trials of life.
- ❏ 7. Clueless about who Jesus is.
- ❏ 8. Often insecure; I always seem to fall into the same old traps, but I have a good heart.
- ❏ 9. A mature woman who has experienced many stages of life, many changes, and many successes as well as failures.
- ❏ 10. A young woman who has never lived alone, never had a job, and never really loved anyone.

❏ 11. An older woman, but a babe in Christ.
❏ 12. One who feels led by God to mentor someone.
❏ 13. Eager to follow, but not ready to lead anyone.
❏ 14. Willing to lead, but overwhelmed by the heavy responsibility of guiding another.
❏ 15. Eager to lead. I realize the responsibility of guiding another and feel able to accept the challenge with God's help.

In the survey above, numbers 1, 4, 7, 10, and 13 indicate you need spiritual guidance for yourself before you mentor. (The best preparation for yourself would be to ask someone to mentor you.)

The numbers 2, 5, 8, 11, and 14 indicate you can be a mentor, but your best days are ahead. (If you chose more than two of these, seek advice from an experienced mentor.)

Checking numbers 3, 6, 12, and 15 indicates your readiness and preparation to mentor. (If you chose at least three of these, you will likely find joy in mentoring.)

Many variables, in addition to spiritual maturity, affect whether the timing is right for you to mentor. Your physical and emotional health, whether you have small children to care for, and your other ministry commitments are all valid and important considerations.

GETTING TO THE HEART OF THE MATTER

Now that you've looked at your general spiritual readiness, it's time to delve a little deeper. The "Heart Search Questionnaire" on the following page will identify attitudes and areas of your life that need peeling and healing. Heart searching can be painful and is best performed from a position of safety as a child of God.

The Lord is your shepherd, the shepherd who searches for you and within you. He searches for what is good and true and exposes what is not.

Read Isaiah 40:11. Picture yourself as the lamb in this scene. Describe what is happening and how you feel.

_____

_____

_____

When I picture that scene I feel safe because Christ holds me so close that I can hear His heartbeat.

Read Isaiah 61:1. Fill in the blanks.

He has sent me to _____ up the _____

Jesus came to *bind* up the *brokenhearted*. I recall how He held me close when I came to Him with a load of shame during one counseling session. I cry when I think about it even now. This prayer describes that experience.

> *"Dear Jesus, when You opened my heart I turned my head away, fearing the stench would cause you to push me away. Instead, you held me close, put salve on my foul wound and said, 'There now, Tricia, don't worry. I'll make it better. You'll see,' and for the first time, I leaned on Your chest and rested."*

As you come to Jesus, pray the following prayer aloud.

> **"Father, You call me now to Your throne—Your throne where love is showered on me, and I fear no retaliation for wrongs I've done or for my immature ways. Illuminate all thoughts and motives where fear, mistrust, and shame distort my thinking, feeling, and choosing. Peel away all that is not true, and call out what is good and pure in me. Reveal my true self, holy and hidden in the life of Your Son, Jesus. Complete this good work in me by the power of Your Holy Spirit. Amen."**

HEART SEARCH QUESTIONNAIRE: A STUDY FROM JAMES

As you read each question and the Scriptures from James beside it, reflect on your life experiences. Then write down a specific example from your life.

1. When have I asked for wisdom, and when was the last time I counseled from truth, not opinion? (James 1:5–6, 3:17)

_____

_____

2. How have I permitted joy to infuse my trials? (1:2)

_____

_____

_____

3. When was the last experience in which I viewed developing perseverance as a worthy purpose of my trial? (1:12)

_____

_____

_____

4. Have I ever blamed God when I was tempted? (1:13)

_____

_____

_____

5. Does this Scripture remind me of a time I failed to speak carefully? (1:19)

_____

_____

_____

6. If I asked a friend or my spouse, "Do I get angry easily?" what would he/she say? (1:19)

_____

_____

7. How has God's truth consistently changed my way of thinking and behaving? (1:21–25)

_____

_____

_____

8. To what degree have I submitted my tongue for God's use? (1:26; 3:1–12)

_____

_____

_____

9. When have I invested myself in ministry to the hurting, lonely, and downtrodden? (1:27)

_____

_____

_____

10. Have I ever shown deference to someone who is important, rich, or of high social stature? (2:1–9)

_____

_____

_____

11. Have I ever felt that God would be more pleased with me if I behave well? (2:10)

_____

_____

_____

12. Have I lived my Christian life more by rules or by constant dependence on Christ? (2:12; 4:6–10)

_____

_____

_____

13. When I noticed someone failing, have I ever judged that person harshly? (2:13; 4:11–12; 5:9)

_____

_____

_____

14. In which areas of my life are there discrepancies between what I say I believe and the way I act? (2:14–26)

_____

_____

_____

15. Have I been jealous of someone and begrudged what that person has or has accomplished? (3:13; 4:1–3)

_____

_____

_____

16. In which ways have I planted seed of righteousness in my life and the lives of others? (3:18)

_____

_____

_____

17. In which ways have I been more preoccupied with things of this world than things of eternal consequence? (4:4; 5:1–5)

_____

_____

_____

18. Is there any sin in my life to which I cling or which I feel unable to conquer? (4:17)

_____

_____

_____

19. In which life situation am I learning how to wait more patiently before the Lord? (5:7–11)

_____

_____

_____

20. If I were to ask my friends if my word could be trusted, what would they say? (5:12)

_____

_____

_____

21. In the past month, when have I interceded in faith before God on behalf of someone emotionally or physically ill? (5:13–15)

_____

_____

_____

22. When did I last practice confession of my sin, according to the Scripture? (5:16)

_____

_____

_____

23. When a brother or sister was straying from the truth, did I respond honestly and lovingly? (5:19–20)

_____

_____

_____

Our prayer for you is that God will honor the desire of your heart to grow in Him. Your completing the Heart Search Questionnaire demonstrates your desire to be a woman after God's own heart. As the Lord reveals attitudes and habits He wishes to remove, open your heart to the Great Physician. Commit yourself to your own healing and wholeness. Many resources are available to you. One excellent book resource is The Search for Significance by Robert S. McGee.

———— Always Remember, Never Forget ————

No blaming, no shaming, just peeling and healing!

CHAPTER FIVE
What Exactly Does a Mentor Do?

You will mentor in a variety of roles according to your merea's need and out of your giftedness.

Some days she may need physical help, other days encouragement. Still, at other times she may need you to simply listen. She may have questions about her security in Christ; she may need a trustworthy friend.

We have grouped mentoring behaviors into five categories: serving, encouraging, teaching, counseling, and guiding. Some behaviors could be logically placed under one category as easily as another. The point is to think about what specifically your merea needs and which role fills that need most closely. In addition, assess your areas of strength as well as areas of needed growth so youcan ask for help, or pursue your own spiritual growth where needed.

MENTORING ROLES
After reading the following role descriptions, do the following exercise:
Place a star (*) beside roles in which you think you will be comfortable.
Place an "x" beside each role which causes you anxiety or fear.

___**Servant:** As a servant, you minister to your merea's needs by offering practical help. Examples may include providing her a ride if she needs it and your schedule permits. Perhaps you will invite her to your home for coffee, requiring some preparation on your part. She may need a connection to another service in the community. Giving her a phone number or offering to accompany her is an act of service. Most importantly, you will minister to her practical needs with authentic humility.

___**Encourager:** When you minister as an encourager, you verbally affirm, support, and cheer on your merea. She needs you in her corner, believing in her. For some women, the mentoring relationship is their first experience in which someone shows confidence in them as a person of precious value.

___**Teacher:**   Share your knowledge of the Lord and Scriptures with your friend. She will most often be spiritually younger, if not chronologically younger. When she misunderstands truth, you will need to clarify for her and sometimes challenge errors in thinking. You may choose to go through a Bible study together.

___**Counselor:**   Chances are, your merea will have many people in her life who give her advice, but few will be able to counsel her with her best interest at heart and with the truth in hand. As you get to know her, you may uncover some old hurts. She will need your nurturing, perhaps even spiritual parenting. Remember: A wise counselor listens more than she talks.

___**Guide:**   You have been where your merea has not yet gone. She needs to see you model the Christian walk so she can follow the path. You will need to model how to fail as much as how to succeed. You also will hold her accountable for growing and living out the goodness of Christ within her.

Review the roles and check the role in which you need to grow the most. Write down at least three actions you will take to strengthen yourself in that area:

_____

_____

_____

_____

EXAMPLES OF MENTORING ROLES

After scanning the mentoring roles described above, write the initial of the role most closely described in the blank of each example below.

S = Servant, E = Encourager, T = Teacher, C = Counselor, G = Guide

___1. "I know this is tough, but I believe in you."

___2. "Yeah, finances are pretty tough for us now, but I tithe still because I've learned through past experience that God is faithful. Let me tell you about it."

___3. "This is what I understand Ephesians 6:1 to mean..."

___4. "It sounds like you are really hurting. Would you like to talk about it? I'd be glad to listen."

___5. "Good for you. I knew you could do it!"

___6. "No, the Scripture does not teach that you must abstain from alcohol to be a Christian. What this passage means is..."

___7. "I know your car is being repaired and you would like to take that Monday night computer class. Could I take you and we can have coffee afterward?"

___ 8. "You asked me to hold you accountable, so the next time we meet, let's talk about how your quiet time is going."

___ 9. "Remember last week when I was telling you about Sandra? I thought about it and realized that I was really unkind. I'm sorry for bringing you into that conversation."

___ 10. "I know of a nonprofit group who might meet your need. May I give you the phone number?"

Although there are no "correct" answers to the list above, the following key shares how we answered them. 1.E, 2.G, 3.T, 4.C, 5.E, 6.T, 7.S, 8.G, 9.G, 10.S. If needed, scan again the descriptions for clue words that may help you more clearly define each role.

GIVING WHAT YOU HAVE RECEIVED

The person best able to mentor as a servant, encourager, teacher, counselor, and guide is the person who has received acts of service, who has received encouragement, and who has received teaching, counseling, and guidance in her Christian walk.

The Lord may choose to minister to you, the mentor, in many ways: through another mentor, through Bible study teachers, through the reading of His Word, or through the support of family and friends. We each need to practice receiving as much as we practice giving.

When you have acknowledged your own needs and thankfully embraced the gifts of service, encouragement, teaching, counseling, and guidance in your own life, you develop a heart attitude of gratefulness, humility, and joy in sharing what you have so richly received. Your heart attitude may be more crucial to your ability to mentor in a role than your expertise.

Receiving from God, often through others, is your best preparation for giving as a mentor. A mentor who is able to give must first receive ministry to her own needs.

RECEIVING ACTS OF SERVICE—Read John 13:8–9. Once Peter understood the necessity of Christ serving him, how did he respond?

_____

_____

_____

Peter received with gratitude. He was humbled by Jesus' loving act of service. An attitude of humility will enable you to serve another.

Read Philippians 2:3–8. Christ performed the most humbling act of service for you when He died on the cross. Does Jesus' suffering and dying for you have an impact on your decision to mentor? If so, in what way?

_____

_____

_____

RECEIVING ENCOURAGEMENT—First Samuel 30:1–19 paints a dismal scene. The Amalekites had burned the city of Ziklag and kidnapped the family members of the Israelite soldiers. The Israelites were so grieved they threatened to stone David, their leader.

Read 1 Samuel 30:6(b) and describe David's response.

_____

_____

The King James Version says, "but David encouraged himself in the LORD his God."

Read 1 Samuel 30:17–19 for the rest of the story. How do you believe that David's stopping to receive encouragement from God affected the outcome of the battle?

_____

_____

_____

Suppose you and your merea have had a misunderstanding. You wonder if the relationship will survive.

In such a time, what actions do you think you may take to encourage yourself in the Lord?

_____

_____

_____

RECEIVING TEACHING—A pastor friend once said, "Lots of people know lots of the Bible and are as mean as the devil about it." Knowledge about the Bible is not the main prerequisite for effectively teaching another.

Read Psalm 25:4–13. Describe the psalmist's attitude.

_____

_____

David bowed his heart and acknowledged that God alone was the source of truth and hope.
What does the Lord promise to those who long to learn His ways (vv. 8–9)?

_____

_____

_____

The Lord promises to guide and teach those who ask for help in understanding His ways. Make yourself a learner before God and humble yourself to learn from others.

RECEIVING WISE COUNSEL—Knowledge and wisdom are both necessary for the mentor. Each plays a unique part in the mentoring relationship. While knowledge is important, wisdom is vital for the person who counsels another.

What do you see as the difference between knowledge and wisdom?

_____

_____

_____

Wisdom is knowledge and understanding applied to daily life. A counselor needs wisdom to meet the needs of someone who has questions or who is in conflict.

Read James 1:5. What can we do to receive wisdom?

_____

_____

_____

_____

Read Isaiah 30:21. How does this verse illustrate God's wise counsel?

This verse says clearly that if you desire to apply God's wisdom in your life, He welcomes you to come to Him and ask with your whole heart.

RECEIVING GUIDANCE—Read John 16:13. Where does a guide go for guidance?

_____

_____

The Holy Spirit is the guide into all truth. Truth is revealed; it is not a recipe to memorize.

What truth about Himself has God revealed or affirmed to you during this study?

_____

_____

_____

As you reflect upon the five roles of a mentor, ask yourself the following questions about your own needs. This season of preparation is your time to grow before you reach out to your merea.

REACHING IN BEFORE REACHING OUT

SERVING

As you think of ways that mentoring may bring you admiration or glory, ask the Lord, "What are the main points of pride in my life which need to be cleansed so I may humbly serve my merea in a way that she will be able to receive ministry from me?"

_____

_____

ENCOURAGING

As you consider the most difficult situation in your life right now, ask the Lord, "What can I do in the midst of this situation to nurture and encourage myself as You would like me to?" What does He bring to mind?

_____

_____

TEACHING

As you consider your need for knowledge of God's Word and God's ways, ask Him, "What one thing do you want me to focus on learning about Your words and Your ways during this time as I prepare to teach another?"

_____

_____

COUNSELING

Speak one of the following prayers as your own:

Lord, I long for Your wisdom. Open my understanding to Your truths and show me how they apply specifically to my life now.

Lord, I want to experience a yearning for Your wisdom. Please align the desire of my heart with Your will.

GUIDANCE
For what situations or needs are you seeking God's guidance now?

_____

_____

_____

_____

_____

What does He want you to know about Himself in each situation you listed?
Stop and ask Him.

_____

_____

_____

_____

_____

_____

_____

_____

In the next chapters, you will take a closer look at each of the roles
described in today's study. Remember to receive ministry to your own needs
while you learn to mentor another.

─────── **Always Remember, Never Forget** ───────

You can give only from what you have received.

CHAPTER SIX
Mentoring as a Servant

I've known a few true servants in my life. My friend, Phil, depicts the true servant heart.

He leaves the parking spaces nearest the church building for visitors on Sundays. He picks up trash on the floor or church grounds, no matter who put it there. And when he leads worship music or teaches Bible study, he demonstrates both confidence and humility.

TWO SIDES OF THE SAME COIN

Most of us think that mentoring means leading. It does. But the other side of the same coin is serving. One way a mentor leads, guides, and nudges a merea forward is by showing love through acts of service. In Christ's life, leading and serving functioned in complete harmony.

Read Mark 8:33. Then read John 13:4–5 and compare. Which Scripture passage describes Jesus taking a strong leadership stance, and which one describes Him in a servant role?

_____

_____

_____

_____

In the passage above, Jesus, with all authority as God, rebuked Peter, saying, "Get behind me, Satan!" because Peter resisted the prospect of Jesus' death as God's plan. Soon after, Jesus was down on His knees washing a day's worth of Jerusalem dirt off Peter's feet.

Review the following list of word descriptions. Write under each heading the words that most closely describe either leading or serving.

		Leading	Serving
strong	guide	_____	_____
correcting	meek	_____	_____
help	kind	_____	_____
humble	decisive	_____	_____

Most often we think of words such as *strong*, *guide*, *decisive*, and *correcting* when we want to describe a leader. Descriptors such as *humble*, *help*, *meek*, and *kind* conjure up an image of a gentle servant. Do you think a person who is a mentor is more often perceived as a leader or a servant?

SERVING ON YOUR KNEES
Read John 13:2. Who does it say would turn against Jesus?

_____

_____

_____

Who had prompted him to betray Jesus?

_____

Thirteen men gathered in an upstairs room to eat what Jesus knew would be their last meal together. Jesus looked around the room and saw not only Peter and His other dearest friends, but also the one who was out to get him. In a few hours his kiss on the cheek would seal Christ's death.

In the drama of that moment, how would you have responded in Jesus' position?

I would have felt:

_____

_____

What I would have done:

_____

_____

_____

I would have screamed, "Unfair!" Maybe I would have thought, "I'm God; I don't have to take this!" and at the nod of my head I would have commanded a battalion of angels to give the traitor what he deserved. Perhaps, knowing I would soon endure the worst agony of all time, I would have obeyed, but despaired.

Jesus did not choose any of these options. He didn't scream. He didn't preach. He didn't balk. He quietly got up from the table, put on a towel, and began washing the disciples' feet. How did He garner the strength to get on His knees and wash feet in that moment?

The secret lies tucked away in two simple words, "Jesus knew" (John 13:3 *Living Bible*). Within these two words lies the strength you need for the task of serving.

One meaning of the word *know* is "to be convinced of" or "to understand." What did Jesus understand that empowered Him to use what He realized would be His last visit with His most-loved friends to teach them how to love one another through serving?

Look at verses John 13:1,3 for the truths Jesus understood that enabled Him to follow through. Complete the following sentences:

Jesus knew that it was _____ for Him to go back to the Father.

Jesus knew that the Father had given Him _____ over everything.

Jesus knew that He had come from _____ and was going back to _____.

Jesus knew the *time* had come for Him to die. He had one more opportunity to show the disciples the meaning of love through an act of service. Jesus knew also that all *power* was His. He understood that just beyond the microcosm of an upstairs room, where thirteen men ate their supper and Satan premeditated murder, God reigned supreme. Jesus saw the big picture. Just as He had come from *God*, He also would return to *God*. The outcome was sure; His future secure. He could obey in the moment knowing God would bring about His purposes however bleak the situation appeared.

Just as Jesus knew His call, you know that God has called you to serve another through mentoring. You want to obey and follow. Know that He has given you power: power to pick up this book; power to say yes; power to embrace the risk. Also know, dear servant, that it is God who will complete the good work as you obey. Knowing that the time is now and the risk is great, do what Jesus did; kneel and wash her feet.

As you prepare to become a true servant, you can deepen your understanding by reading Improving Your Serve by Charles Swindoll.

SERVING AS A MAJOR DOMO

In Victorian England well-to-do families had servants who were confidantes as well as purchasing agents. They served as the liaison between the lady and the community, bringing her food, clothes, and furniture. She rarely shopped in commercial stores. Her chief domestic servant, a major domo, worked tirelessly to provide all the resources she needed for her and her family to live in abundance. This special servant linked the wealthy woman to life.

Read John 14:16–17. To what resource did Jesus link His disciples?

_____

_____

I traveled to a small, country health clinic to gather survey data for a research project. All day long, I explained to clients how to complete the 110 questions on the survey. The day moved faster than the respondents did, and I became frustrated knowing I had a deadline to meet. Late in the afternoon, I approached Myra, a woman about my age, to complete the survey. She hesitated. Obviously embarrassed, she said, "I can't read." Distracted from the pressure of my research, I asked, "How did it happen, Myra?" She said, "When I was little my parents thought I was retarded, so they never taught me or cared about my schooling. So later I never thought I could. Now, I'm too old to learn."

Jot down some ways you, as a mentor servant, might respond to Myra's needs.

_____

_____

SERVING WHEN THE EGGS BLOW UP

In the following months after meeting Myra, I served her by connecting her with community resources which could help her learn to read. I often sloshed through the mud to her home to encourage her, check her progress, and see what I could do to help. One day Myra proudly told me, "I'm so excited. I read a book to my little boy." That's all it took.

If I were the type to make excuses, I would explain that I left the eggs to boil for three hours due to extenuating circumstances. I was in a hurry to get to church and donned my panty hose only to find a hole in them. Knowing the culprit was my 15-year-old daughter, I insisted she give me her holeless pair which were now already on her legs. After the frantic panty hose switch, I ran out the door to church, without one look back at the steaming eggs. I was distracted, okay?

But since I'm not one to make excuses, let's just say that when I came out of church three hours later, I found a note on my windshield, written by my husband, Randy, who had gone home earlier to change clothes for work. The note read, "The eggs are done." (My husband has a gift for understatement.)

I dreaded going home and was relieved to find Randy had already gone to work. He was thoughtful enough to leave me a note on the garage door: "The smell is part of what is left of the six eggs. I let out most of the smoke and cleaned up what I could. I will finish the kitchen ceiling if you can finish the walls and floor." His drawing (yes, he actually drew a picture!) showed in graphic detail exactly how far the exploding eggs had traveled—from the kitchen, over an archway, through the living room and dining area, dropping just in time to splatter on the back door.

My husband could've fussed; he could've shamed me; he could've become angry or in his best parental tone lectured me about the danger of fire. But he didn't. He cleaned up what he could and brought a little humor into the situation.

In your mentoring relationship as well as in life, things may not go as planned. In fact, that's a guarantee. Your merea fizzles out on a Bible study that you and she started together. Family needs conflict with commitments you made to the mentoring relationship. Kids act up. You argue with your spouse. In short, the eggs explode.

When you get discouraged and your servant's heart is just about to give out, remember you're not alone there scraping egg goo off the back door. Jesus knows. And He's not lecturing you or asking you why you can't get your act together. With His help, clean up what you can and find someone who will laugh with you about the oddities of life. Now then, it's your serve.

—————— **Always Remember, Never Forget** ——————

True servants have dirty knees (sometimes even covered with egg goo).

CHAPTER SEVEN
Mentoring as an Encourager

I did not understand what happened that night. I still don't. I just know God used me as an encourager to save a life.

Just a few weeks before, I had survived one of the darkest periods of my life: a broken engagement to a man I believed was sent from God to me. Not only had I experienced the pain of loss, but also I was feeling the humiliation of a failed relationship.

As I prepared to speak to a small group of Christian women in the YMCA in our little town, God seemed to be nudging me to speak on brokenheartedness. Because I have a sanguine, always-happy personality, I refused to admit I had even experienced brokenheartedness. I certainly was not going to tell anyone how broken and humiliated I was! All through that afternoon I struggled with God's will. He kept leading me back to Isaiah 61:1, "The Spirit of the Sovereign Lord is on me, because the Lord has anointed me to preach good news to the poor. He has sent me to bind up the brokenhearted." The words seemed magnified on the page of my Bible. I kept reminding God of who I was (as if He had not created me just as I am!):

"Lord, remember me? I'm the 'Joy girl'! How about Philippians 4?"

"No. Isaiah 61."

"I could wax eloquent for hours on 'I can do all things through Him who strengthens me' " (Phil. 4:13).

"No."

"But I could really tell how wonderful You are, expounding on 'My God shall supply all your need according to his riches in glory by Christ Jesus' " (v. 19, KJV).

"No. How about the needs of those who are broken? Isaiah 61."

"But, You know me, Lord. I can't talk about brokenheartedness. I don't know enough about it."

"That's a lie. You know a lot about brokenheartedness."

"Rejoice in the Lord, always: and again I say, Rejoice" (v. 4).

"And again I say, brokenheartedness. Isaiah 61."

"O, God! Don't make me be obedient to this humiliation. I beg you. What good will it do?"

Nevertheless, receiving no bolt of lightning or handwriting on the wall to change my direction, I spoke to the women that night about brokenheartedness. I told the whole story of how God had led me through the dark hours of the breakup, giving back the ring, returning shower gifts, throwing away invitations and a wedding dress. After the session, I avoided conversation and headed for my car. As I drove home, I looked up into a dark, cold sky. I had never felt so alone.

"Well, Lord, I hope you're satisfied. What good did that do? I humiliated myself in front of a bunch of catty women in my own hometown. Thank goodness I did not know all of them."

The next day I received this word from a woman who had attended the session:

"You don't know me, but I slipped into the conference room last night at the Y. I had gone there to buy a membership for my little son, the last gift to him from a desperate mother about to commit suicide. I had returned a diamond ring to the man of my dreams that afternoon. His rejection was the last one in a long line of rejections. I just had nowhere to turn. I was brokenhearted.

But I heard you say, 'If you are brokenhearted, listen to this: It doesn't matter if no man ever puts his arms around you and tells you he loves you; you can lean on the Everlasting Arms.' I decided to do that. I trusted Jesus as my Savior. And you know what? I believe through you God saved my earthly life and my life for eternity in heaven. What joy I found! Thank you for being an encourager."

THE ENCOURAGER WITHIN

While most encouraging words don't save someone's life in the literal sense, they certainly breathe life into frustration, hopelessness, and despair. Some people are natural encouragers. They make everyone feel good about themselves by smiling and affirming them verbally. We surveyed 200 women, asking them to choose from eight options what they viewed as the main role of a mentor. Fifty percent of them identified support/encouragement as the main role of a mentor.

List some ways people have encouraged you.

_____

_____

Perhaps you are not a natural encourager. You may find it difficult to praise verbally or to hug your merea. You can encourage her by sharing your passion for life, in whichever area God has allowed it to flourish. Something as simple as a high-five can lift her spirits.

Find the italicized high-five words in the word search puzzle and circle each one. The words may run up, down, across, or diagonal:

The High-Five List

a *smile*
a *hug*
a *compliment* on clothes or physical attributes
sharing an encouraging *Scripture*
prayer with her or for her
verbal *affirmation* in front of others
praise for her effort, growth, or job well done
writing a *letter* to *encourage* her

A	C	O	M	P	L	I	M	E	N	T
P	F	F	L	K	J	T	E	P	R	R
R	E	F	F	S	R	S	M	I	L	E
A	L	M	I	C	C	C	X	T	T	N
I	L	O	P	R	A	Y	E	R	T	R
S	U	G	Y	I	M	E	R	E	R	E
E	I	T	G	P	T	A	E	E	L	T
K	C	U	S	T	E	P	T	M	R	T
R	H	W	S	U	U	T	N	I	T	E
P	R	O	L	R	E	R	R	T	O	L
S	M	I	O	E	L	N	G	T	I	N

THE VISION OF VICTORY

The Old Testament tells a story about a woman who envisioned victory for her merea and supported him until the victory became reality.

Read Judges 4:1–4 and 6–8. Why do you think Barak asked Deborah to go into battle with him?

_____

Barak lacked confidence or was afraid. We all need someone to believe in us and stand by our sides in a difficult situation.

Look again at verse 6. How did Deborah call her merea, Barak, to action and remind him of God's promise?

_____

_____

_____

Deborah saw great promise in Barak. She believed he could do whatever God had called him to do. Part of encouraging your merea is believing she is worthy, reminding her of God's promises, and then nudging her to action. At times, you may need to call her to accomplish some hard things, to fight some battles against bondage (to drugs, poor habits, a haunting past).

Read Judges 4:9. Record what Deborah did to help Barak.

_____

_____

_____

The Scripture says that Deborah agreed to go with Barak for support. Mentors walk alongside their mereas, sometimes going physically to help them walk the walk, not just talk the talk.

Do you think it was convenient for Deborah to stop what she was doing? How does her commitment to supporting Barak apply to you as a mentor?

_____

_____

Her decision required her to stop what she was doing and lay aside her own interests to accompany him. The truth is, mentoring requires commitment: commitment to God, commitment to yourself, commitment to your merea.

Read Judges 4:14. List ways you could cheer on your merea as Deborah cheered on Barak.

_____

_____

THE REALITY OF VICTORY

Read Judges 4:23–24. What evidence do you find that Deborah followed through with her commitment to support Barak to the point of victory?

_____

_____

The Scriptures record that Barak, with Deborah's support, defeated Jabin and his army.

One valuable way to encourage a merea is to praise her for her effort—even baby steps—and rejoice with her in successes. Look for and celebrate all moments of victory in your merea's life and walk with Christ.

Read aloud the following victory song of Deborah and Barak in Judges 5:1–3:

"On that day Deborah and Barak son of Abinoam sang this song:
*'When the princes in Israel take the lead,
When the people willingly offer themselves—praise the Lord!
I will sing to the Lord, I will sing:
I will make music to the Lord, the God of Israel.' "*

Deborah envisioned victory long before it became reality. Ponder what you might like to see happen in your merea's life as an outgrowth of your mentoring. Describe it here.

_____

_____

_____

Praise God for your vision of hope. Ask Him to begin even now to bring to pass what you have envisioned for your merea. Once in the mentoring relationship, let your merea hear you praying over her, praising God for her. You are an instrument of encouragement.

──────── **Always Remember, Never Forget** ────────

Every woman needs a friend to stand by her side and
believe in her. Be that friend.

CHAPTER EIGHT
Mentoring as a Teacher

One Sunday afternoon Becky, a single mother and member of my new Christians class, rushed into my home.

"Okay, where is the list?" she said.

"What list?"

"The list of things Christians don't do. And don't tell me about those Ten Commandments. What I need isn't there!"

"What do you need?"

"The list! There *is* a list of no-nos, isn't there? For starters, where does it say, *No smoking*? This morning after that long church service," (It had lasted 55 minutes; pretty short, I thought), Becky said, "I lit a cigarette in the lobby, and you'd have thought I committed murder. Four people pounced on me."

"Oh, Becky, I'm sorry. I thought you knew we don't allow smoking in the church building."

"Well, I guess I know that one now! One woman said to her husband, 'Those miniskirts are bad enough, but we draw the line at smoking.' "

Becky demanded I show her where the Bible listed rules on miniskirts, cursing, smoking, and using cocaine. She feared that behaviors which seemed normal to her would blow the socks off "good" members! Reluctantly, I told her there was no official list of things Christians don't do. Living the Christian life involves more than following a list of dos and don'ts.

I contemplated how best to begin teaching Becky. I developed a plan based on five questions: What should I teach her—what did she most need at that time? Where should I teach her—at her home, my home, or a neutral location? When should I teach her—would I know when the time was right? How should I teach—how could I present the information in a way she could receive it? Why should I teach her—was it really that important to take the time and effort the task was going to require?

WHAT DO I TEACH?

Becky and I made a contract. She promised to be patient and work on one behavior at a time. I promised to teach her three things: God's Word, as I had experienced it; church culture, so she could fulfill her role of edifying the church with her God-given gifts; and life principles, based on what God had taught me in life.

TEACHING GOD'S WORD

Becky did not expect me to be a theologian. I felt inadequate to teach anyone God's Word, but I was light-years ahead of her. I felt inadequate only because I had compared myself to an old, revered Sunday School teacher I had known for years.

God did not expect me to be like my teacher. He expected me to share meaningful verses I knew from personal experience, not the thousands of verses I didn't know. I simply told Becky what God had shown me in His Word. We began studying Colossians 3. I told her how I had approached each of these areas, as God led. Later we studied other passages.

Read Colossians 3:1,5–10. From the forbidden behaviors mentioned in the passage, choose three behaviors to record in the left column. Then, on the right, restate each one in a positive way, like the example given.

God Forbids	God's Best for Me
sexual immorality	sexual purity—freedom from guilt
_____	_____
_____	_____
_____	_____

The most effective way to teach the truths above is to share with your merea that God does not intend to prohibit fun and joy, but to give to His children what is best.

TEACHING CHURCH CULTURE

Review the following activities some Christians would forbid. In the middle column, write where you heard this rule. In the third column, give your opinion.

"THE LIST"	Where I Heard This	Your Opinion
1. Dancing	_____	_____
2. Smoking	_____	_____
3. Wearing pants to church	_____	_____
4. Playing cards	_____	_____
5. Drinking alcohol	_____	_____

6. Other _____ _____ _____

Every church has an unspoken culture. The purpose of talking with your merea about your denominational and church culture and expectations is not so much to identify sinful behavior as it is to help her feel comfortable in knowing what to expect. I gave tips on accepted attire, words to say and not to say, and supported her as she developed her own convictions about issues on "THE LIST."

In addition, I taught her ways that she could discover her spiritual gifts, using them to build up the church. Remember this: every church member has a job to do or a talent to use in the church. God planned it that way. Even Becky, a babe in Christ, had potential for uplifting our church. (When I first told her that, she laughed. To tell the truth, I hardly believed it myself!) Her exuberant joy in a newfound Lord was contagious among our members. Using tact and socially-accepted habits (most of the time!), she helped them see how to reach people who didn't fit in.

TEACHING LIFE PRINCIPLES

I also taught Becky ordinary things God had taught me about life. As a widow, I shared what I had learned as a single parent: how to find godly examples for my son, how to lead painless family devotionals, how to balance career and home, how to remain a loving mother (on days you want to kill your children), and how to practice good money management. I believe God lets us experience certain things in life which prepare us to help others in their spiritual walk.

List some things you have learned from your life experiences that may be helpful to your merea.

_____

_____

_____

WHEN DO I TEACH?
Jesus taught in a variety of locations. Read the following verses and record each place you find Him teaching.

1. Luke 19:47; John 8:2   In the _____
2. Mark 10:1   On a _____
3. Matthew 5:1–2   On the side of a _____
4. Luke 5:3; Matt 13:2   In a _____

HOW DO I TEACH?

Jesus taught everywhere—in the temple, on a riverbank, on the side of a mountain, and in a boat. Where can you teach your merea? Think of several suitable places which provide a quiet teaching environment and list them here.

_____

_____

_____

Living a godly Christian life is more often caught than taught. Don't be surprised if your merea learns as much in everyday experiences with you as when you sit down for a Bible study. Be alert for the "teachable moment." It involves watching for readiness and giving what is needed more than planning a two-hour study.

Tricia's mom illustrated this point with Emily, Tricia's seven-year-old daughter. As Emily and "Mimi" read a book about Emily's favorite painter, Vincent Van Gogh (she was fascinated that he cut off his ear!), Emily pointed out to Mimi that Van Gogh was very poor and that his talent was never recognized until after he died.

Mimi asked, "So Emily, if he wasn't famous, and no one bought his paintings, why do you think he kept on painting?"

Emily replied, "Cause it was just in him. It was his life."

Mimi said, "That's right. It was just in him. God gave him this talent. He couldn't *not* paint. It made him happy."

Mimi used Emily's readiness to drop in a profound spiritual truth: talent is God-given and is to be honored, not for external rewards, but because it brings joy to the heart. Look for the teachable moment.

Jesus used a variety of teaching methods to drive home a point. Sometimes He illustrated spiritual truths using familiar life situations; other times He helped people learn by doing, like when Peter walked on the water.

Check the following teaching methods you would most likely use.

- ❏ Illustrating or using word pictures
- ❏ Sharing personal experience
- ❏ Showing how to do something
- ❏ Giving a book and assigning reading
- ❏ Listening to a cassette tape
- ❏ Your ideas: _____

How you will teach also refers to the attitudes you bring to the teaching experience. More than using a variety of teaching methods, a loving attitude determines how much learning takes place.

**Complete the questionnaire below, reflecting on your level of "loving-
ness."**

THE LOVING TEACHER

**Listed below are five traits of a loving teacher. Beneath each trait, check
the descriptions which most apply to you.**

1. A loving teacher knows her textbook.

   ❏ I study my Bible diligently.
   ❏ I'm too busy to study regularly.
   ❏ I search the Scriptures for truths to apply in my life.
   ❏ I want to study more, but never seem to get around to it.

2. A loving teacher shows her student how to study.

   ❏ I don't know how to study my Bible, much less how to show someone
   else.
   ❏ I can show, step-by-step, how to get the most from God's Word.
   ❏ I can show her how to use study aids (concordances, commentaries).
   ❏ I'll need help to grow enough to teach another how to study.

3. A loving teacher matches her student's pace.

   ❏ I'm easily frustrated with slow learners.
   ❏ I need rapid, visible results to feel I'm accomplishing something.
   ❏ I'm able to set aside my plan in order to focus on what is important to
   her.
   ❏ I'm comfortable with learning that is "two steps forward, three steps
   back."

4. A loving teacher accepts her student, even when she doesn't bring apples.

   ❏ I have difficulty continuing to minister when someone acts ungrateful.
   ❏ I'm able to affirm her, even when she's angry or dissatisfied with me.
   ❏ I can accept her unlovely traits.
   ❏ I'd be tempted to criticize her to others if she doesn't seem to learn
   from me.

5. A loving teacher provides accountability for her student.

❑ I will keep my promises because I am as accountable to her as she is to me.

❑ I can lovingly confront her when she doesn't keep commitments.

❑ I look forward to graduation day, when I'm not responsible for her growth.

❑ How she follows through and grows is her business; I won't check on her.

WHY DO I TEACH?

Above all, a mentor is a hope-giver. One December my daughter Patsy, a seventh-grade teacher, received gifts from her students. Latisha, the poorest girl in the class, said, "Miz Farmer, I don't have no Christmas present for you, but I'll give you a hug." Tears rolled down Patsy's cheeks. As they embraced, she felt God's presence.

"Mom," Patsy said, "I told God I would hug Latisha every day. I wasn't there to teach math, but to encourage a fragile ego, with a fragmented family in a housewithout water. She needed hope, and I was determined to give it."

Whenever you teach you are not just sharing information, you are sharing hope. Why will you teach?

———— Always Remember, Never Forget ————

Apples or no apples, love her.

CHAPTER NINE
Mentoring as a Counselor

If the idea of counseling causes you to shake in your electric blue, three-inch spiked heels, you are not alone.

Most of us believe we are not qualified. Only years of training can prepare someone to counsel. Right?

Psychologist Larry Crabb writes in his book *Connecting*, "We need folks who can talk to us wisely and sensitively and meaningfully about our deepest battles....That person may or may not be a trained professional." What a blessing to hear these words from a "trained professional."

THE NEED AND THE CALL
What qualifies you, then, to counsel?

1. **The need**—The need for godly counsel among Christians far outweighs the number of trained professionals available to provide it. When 176 women responded to the question, "Have you ever felt a need for a mentor?" almost 85 percent said "yes." Many expressed a longing for someone to share with and to lean on.

2. **The call**—Jesus calls you to the ministry of burden-bearing.

Read Galatians 6:2. List examples of burdens your merea may share with you.

_____

_____

_____

Burdens you may encounter include relationship difficulties, death of a loved one, physical illness, personal self-worth issues, and questions about child-rearing.

Now read below Galatians 6:2 as it appears in the Amplified Bible, and respond to the question.

"Bear (endure, carry) one another's burdens and troublesome moral faults. . .."

In addition to challenging life experiences, what else must you bear with your merea?

t _____ m _____ f _____

I'm holey, how about you? Every person I know has holes in her holiness just as I do. We all have annoying, immature faults. (Just ask anyone who's been married for more than 20 minutes.) Jesus calls you to bear the moral inconsistencies of a growing, sometimes floundering, child of God in process.

3. The life of Christ in you—Larry Crabb asserts that the person best qualified to engage with someone at the deepest levels of need is "the person most filled with the energy of Christ." Your living, growing, all-consuming relationship with Jesus Christ is your strongest qualification to counsel another.

Describe evidence in your life that your relationship with Jesus Christ is:

Living

_____

_____

Growing

_____

_____

All-consuming

_____

_____

A COUNSELOR IS SOMEONE WHO. . .

If you are reading this book, your desire to mentor probably grows from a caring heart. But is that quality alone enough to equip you to counsel another? Let's ask the question another way.

Recall your deepest hurts, fears, and failures. What kind of a person would you feel free to share your deepest hurts with?

Below, list the characteristics of a person with whom you would share these thoughts and feelings.

I would look for someone who:

_____

_____

_____

_____

_____

Here's my list. I would look for someone who:

    ... *has endured life struggles and crises.*

    ... *is humble (doesn't think she is better than I am), gentle, and compassionate.*

    ... *keeps a confidence (doesn't need to impress others with knowing the "inside scoop").*

    ... *knows and shares truth (not just what I want to hear) with my spiritual welfare as her concern.*

    ... *sees and calls out what is pure and holy in me (even when it's hidden very well).*

    ... *loves me—accepts me, warts and all, while sharing God's vision for me.*

    ... *is slow to give advice—more concerned with the process than quick answers.*

    ... *listens intently to me—hears beneath the words.*

    ... *speaks from who she is, not from degrees or credentials.*

    ... *won't leave when I behave badly or fail miserably.*

    ... *loves Jesus Christ more than my approval.*

After studying the lists above, ask yourself, "Am I that kind of person?" A rather tall order, isn't it?

WHAT COUNSELING IS AND IS NOT

Recently, a dear friend was hurt by spiteful words of another person. Seeing the tears in her eyes made me feel angry that someone had mistreated her. As she shared the experience, I listened intently, internally boiling.

Finally I blurted, "What did you say after she said those rude things?" Before she could answer, I forged ahead in a "vengeance is mine" mode and said, "I would have felt like slapping her!"

Once I had stopped foaming at the mouth, inhaled deeply, and straightened my halo, I approached my friend and said, "I don't think my response to your hurt was very helpful. I was just riding your wave. Sorry about that." I had overreacted, failed to address her feelings because I was so caught up in my own emotion, and provided the perfect illustration of what counseling is not.

Review the following list of behaviors often connected with counseling. Check the three behaviors which, in your opinion, are most useful for the counselor.

❑   a. Standing in someone's corner shouting, "Sic 'em!" (Hint: That's what I did in the illustration.)

❑   b. Listening intently

❑   c. Speaking truthful, loving words

❑   d. Knowing and sharing answers to problems

❑   e. Pursuing your own intimate, passionate relationship with Christ

❑   f. Memorizing the right Scripture verses for most major life problems

DEFINING THE ROLE OF COUNSELOR

Which items did you mark? I marked b., c., and e. as the most useful to the counselor. You probably already guessed a. was not useful. When you counsel, be careful to avoid surfing on someone else's wave of emotion. While empathy for another's hurts is helpful, empathy is best shown by listening *intently*. True listening requires skill and commitment but is probably the most desired attribute of a wise counselor. After listening, speaking *truthful, loving* words is the means by which the life of Christ is infused from your heart to another's *heart*. Requiring yourself to know and share the answers to problems may prevent you from listening (because you are desperately thinking of the "right" answer), and may impair your merea's ability to search out her own truth. Go carefully here. You may never know the right Scripture for most of life's problems. Even if you did, your merea does not need Scripture recitation; she needs the truth of His Word revealed through the life of someone who is honestly pursuing her own *intimate, passionate* relationship with the Savior.

Now that we have described what counseling is and is not, let's define the term. In its most narrow definition, counselor means "advisor." For our purposes, we will define counselor in a new way.

Scan the paragraph just before the heading above for clues, then complete the following sentence.

A counselor is someone who, out of a heart sensitive to God, and an

_____, _____ relationship with Christ, with compassion

listens _____, and speaks _____, _____ words to

_____ another, and in so doing, infuses life, healing, and hope into

the _____ of another person.

A counselor must have an intimate, passionate relationship with Christ. She listens intently, and speaks truthful, loving words. Through listening and speaking she infuses life, healing, and hope into the heart of her merea.

The Lost Art of Listening

Why listen? It's good for you as well as your merea. One study showed that during talking, blood pressure increases slightly, as compared with the blood pressure while being quiet. Interestingly, during listening, blood pressure drops significantly, not only below readings taken during talking, but also below the blood pressure recorded during quiet times. So listen and lower your blood pressure!

As for the benefits to your merea, paying close attention to her verbal and nonverbal messages affirms her as a person of value. Your listening also gives her time to become aware of what she is thinking and feeling.

If listening is so valuable, why don't we do it more and better? Listening is often misunderstood. Often we think of it as being synonymous with hearing. It isn't. We also tend to think of listening as dry, boring, and passive. On the contrary, listening is hard work. Proactive listening requires you to choose consciously to focus on and seek to understand the meaning of the internal experience your merea is expressing verbally.

When you don't listen well, what are some of the reasons? Check the distractions that most often impair your listening.

❏ 1. I'm thinking of what to say next.

❏ 2. I'm busy evaluating the rightness or wrongness of what is being said.

❑ 3. I am uncomfortable with silence; I tend to fill in the blank spots.

❑ 4. I am sometimes too tired to focus.

❑ 5. It's hard to pay attention (this could range from true attention deficit problems to simply being distracted about matters of everyday life).

❑ 6. If I don't like the subject matter, I just tune out.

The first step in becoming a more active and focused listener is becoming aware of the distractions that are most likely to pull you away from the conversation. All skills improve with practice. Look individually at each item you checked and work on it in your everyday conversations.

PREPARING YOURSELF AS A COUNSELOR

Counseling requires more than a caring heart, although that is a good beginning.
Listed below are actions you can take to prepare yourself to counsel.

Read each statement and complete the activity.

1. Ask God for His wisdom.

Read James 1:5 and fill in the blanks.

"But if any of you lacks _____ he should _____ God."

Asking God acknowledges Him as the source of wisdom, instead of depending solely on your own intellect and reasoning powers.

2. Be aware of your own limitations.

You cannot know all the answers for problems, and you should give out advice carefully. Use the resources and support available to help you discern when it's time to consult someone with more skill or to refer your merea to other resources for help.

3. Intentionally develop skills useful in counseling.

Develop your listening skills and other communication skills by practicing during everyday conversation. Study books such as *Wise Counsel* by J. Drakeford and C. King, *Telling Each Other the Truth* by W. Backus, *Connecting* by L. Crabb, and *Communication* by H. Harral.

4. Acknowledge the Holy Spirit as the sole source of truth, healing, and hope for the human condition.

Read John 16:13–16. Ask Him to purify your desires for personal glory so that you may be a usable vessel.

5. Get to know Christ better by searching the Scriptures. Talk to Him all day.

Read 1 Kings 19:11–13. After talking, what can you do to receive God's message?

_____

_____

_____

_____

Elijah learned that the Lord often speaks in a "still, small voice." To hear Him, quiet your heart and listen with your spirit.

─────── **Always Remember, Never Forget** ───────

A counselor listens a lot, talks a little, and prays while doing both.

CHAPTER TEN
Mentoring as a Guide

An important part of being a mentor is serving as a guide—physical, social, emotional—and most of all, a spiritual guide.

Probably the most important guide in the Old Testament was Moses, who guided Israel from Egypt to the promised land, Palestine. Moses was a mentor to Joshua, who also became a great leader.

"Am I going to have to be a pillar of fire or a big cloud if I guide someone as a mentor? Not me, sister!"

Wait! Before you think Moses and Joshua were bigger than life, just remember, they were ordinary men. They performed great feats because of one thing: they served God wholeheartedly (Num. 32:11–12).

Think of some changes you will need to make in order to serve God wholeheartedly. Write in your own words your promise to God of wholehearted devotion.

_____

_____

GUIDE HER TO SPIRITUAL CLOSENESS WITH GOD

I have always believed that Moses alone saw the face of God when God gave him the tablets at the top of Mt. Sinai. However, as I searched the Scriptures for this book, I learned something new about the relationship between Moses and Joshua.

Read Exodus 24:12–13 and 32:15–18. What evidence do you find that Joshua may have accompanied his mentor, Moses, near the mountaintop to receive the Ten Commandments?

_____

_____

In Exodus 24:12–13 God invited Moses to go up the mountain. Moses took Joshua as his aide, while elders waited below. Just how far Joshua traveled with Moses is not known. Regardless, Joshua was close to Moses when he received the Commandments. The mentor/merea relationship was so intimate that Moses took Joshua with him through the most momentous experience of his life!

GUIDE HER BY MODELING THE ROLE
Read Exodus 33:7–11. What impact did Moses' relationship with God make on Joshua?

_____

_____

_____

Moses lived out his relationship with God before Joshua. He modeled the role. Joshua patterned his relationship with God after Moses to the extent that when Moses commissioned another person to lead the people of Israel, he chose Joshua.

Moses modeled not only how to succeed, but also how to fail. When in anger he struck the rock before the people of Israel, instead of verbally commanding the water to come forth as God instructed, God prohibited him from entering the land of Canaan. We may think God judged him harshly, considering His consistent obedience throughout the rest of his life. But Moses had also experienced God in a way no other man had (Deut. 34:10), so God expected implicit trust from him. However, even in failure Moses modeled the honorable way to live. Not once in Scripture do we find him casting a shadow of doubt on God's goodness because he didn't get the thing he wanted most in his life: to enter the promised land.

Think of a painful failure in your life. Have you forgiven yourself? Without sharing the actual experience, what truths did you learn which would be helpful to your merea?

_____

_____

_____

_____

GUIDE HER WHERE YOU'VE BEEN

A guide can only take someone where she herself has been. As you guide your merea, consider the biblical example of Joshua, who scouted a new territory to which, one day, he would guide a nation.

Read Numbers 13:1–2, then the verses listed on the next page, also from Numbers 13. Write in the middle column what Joshua and Caleb did to accomplish the tasks on the left. In the right column list what you can do as a guide to apply these truths in your mentoring relationship (*Hoshea* in vv. 8,16 is Joshua).

Tasks Accomplished	What Joshua and Caleb Did	What I Can Do
1.(v.17) Get on a higher plane for a better perspective on life.	_____ _____ _____ _____	_____ _____ _____ _____
2.(v. 18) Know the background of the people.	_____ _____ _____ _____	_____ _____ _____ _____
3.(v. 19) Scout the territory for barriers.	_____ _____ _____	_____ _____ _____
4.(v. 20, 23–24) Plan for rich harvest.	_____ _____ _____ _____	_____ _____ _____ _____
5.(v. 26) Show accountability.	_____ _____ _____ _____	_____ _____ _____ _____
6.(v. 27) Encourage.	_____ _____	_____ _____

7. (v. 28) Be realistic.

_____ _____
_____ _____
_____ _____
_____ _____
_____ _____
_____ _____

8. (Numbers 13:30; 14:6–8)
   Trust God.

_____ _____
_____ _____
_____ _____
_____ _____

9. (Numbers 14:9) Depend
   on God for courage.

_____ _____
_____ _____
_____ _____
_____ _____

Joshua and the other guides traveled up into hill country to get a better perspective. As you mentor, do what you need to do to get a "hill perspective": participate in a prayer retreat or spiritual renewal—individually or with your church group. Don't forget to ask your prayer partner to pray for you daily.

Joshua scouted out the territory. He studied the background of the people in the land (were they strong? weak?). Get to know your merea: her hometown, her family, and her interests will tell you much about who she is and will help you mentor her in an appropriate way. Get to know her personality traits, too. You will then be better prepared to meet her needs.

Joshua also found out if the towns were walled. You, too, will need to assess for barriers in the relationship. Then plan a strategy to overcome them. Look for barriers you may have erected also. Let go of defensiveness.

Joshua brought back fruit; it was the season to harvest grapes. What kind of harvest do you envision for your mentoring relationship?

Joshua and the scouts reported to Moses, Aaron, and all the people. Design a way to be accountable to each other and to the church and/or the Christian community around you.

Joshua encouraged Moses and the Israelites back in camp when he reported the land of "milk and honey." Even with this glowing report, the scouts acknowledged that the cities were walled, with large, strong warriors. After assessing both the blessings to be gained as well as the risks involved, Caleb, in faith, recommended they move ahead. Be decisive, and encourage new opportunities   or newfound capabilities in your merea.

Before they entered the land, Joshua and Caleb humbled themselves and vowed to trust God. They were not fearful because they depended on God.

Psalm 139:9–10 reads: "If I settle on the far side of the sea, even there your hand will guide me." Memorize Scripture verses like this one to share with your merea as she crosses into new territory. Why don't you memorize this one right now?

Fill in these blanks without looking at the lines above.

"If I _____ on the _____ of the _____ , even there _____ will _____ me" (Psalm ____ :9– __).

Do not fear failure in mentoring. God is with you. Pause now and thank Him for His presence in your life.

GUIDE HER BY BEING THERE FOR HER

Did you ever go to a Saturday matinee as a child and watch a western hero in action? Bandits may have placed him in imminent danger in every scene, but just when he needed it, a scout or guide would show up standing on a high mesa overlooking the threatening scene below. A mentor is like that: just when you need her most, she is there.

As a child I had a mentor, Miss Jamie, who was my Sunbeam leader when I was a five-year-old. When I was in sixth grade, she led our church missions group when no one would take responsibility for guiding us. When I was a young mother, Jamie came back into my life as a guide in missions activities. It seemed that just when I needed her to shape my life, she was always there. She gave me independence from time to time, but she was always there to nudge me along when I needed help.

Recently, I visited my alma mater, where one of my former students is a professor. She said to me, "You pop up periodically in my life as a mentor and guide." That's exactly my feeling toward Jamie. How can you be there guiding your merea when she needs you, taking responsibility for her spiritual safety, offering guidelines and boundaries just as Jamie, Moses, or Joshua served as guides for others?

As you prepare to guide another, take a moment to read aloud the following prayer:

Guide Me

Lord, I'm out here on the point
Looking for Your perfect way.
And I'm praying You'll anoint,
Help me guide her day by day.

*Help me know North, South, East, West;
Directions which You plan to give.
Let me guide her to the best,
Show her how to serve and live.*

—©1998 Edna Ellison

─────── **Always Remember, Never Forget** ───────

You can only guide someone where you've been.

CHAPTER ELEVEN
Taking Off the Mask

One of the most poignant scenes in children's literature appears in *The Velveteen Rabbit* when the stuffed rabbit asks the Skin Horse, "What is REAL?"

"Real isn't how you are made," said the Skin Horse. "It's a thing that happens to you."

"Does it hurt?"

"Sometimes."

"Does it happen all at once?"

"It doesn't happen all at once. You become."

How do we become real when the whole world is demanding that we perform according to someone else's standard, no matter what the cost? Dr. C. Anne Davis once said in a conference that unwritten social mores in America demand a facade between strangers and us. Davis calls this outer layer our public layer. We keep our public layer in place to hide our true selves. In fact, we use ritual greetings such as, "How are you?" when we really don't want to know specific details about how someone is. Actually, she says, we "establish closeness to keep us apart." The social distance gives us the safety space we need.

Years ago, psychologist Abraham Maslow created a graphic visual to illustrate human needs. He placed love, security, and other needs on tiers of a triangle. The lower levels dealt with issues of self-preservation, such as physical and safety needs. The highest level of need was "self-actualization" (we might call it "self-fulfillment"). He suggested that every person started at the bottom of the triangle trying to meet his needs. Only when that level's need was met could the individual progress upward to pursue meeting the next higher level of needs.

Self-preservation can be a strong motivator of behavior. Even normally unacceptable behavior for the sake of self-preservation is often justified. For instance, if someone is assaulting another person, the law agrees that self-defense is justified, even if it harms the perpetrator. When we wear an external facade, we are trying to meet our basic human need for love and acceptance by being what we think others expect of us.

From the following statements, identify those behaviors which characterize a person who is wearing a mask (m), a person who is real (r), or one about which you are not sure (ns).

_____ 1. The church copy machine stopped working while Sandra was using it. She doesn't want to be blamed and decides not to tell anyone.

_____ 2. Juanita has two very good friends. She talks to each woman about what she dislikes about the other.

_____ 3. Patricia calls Martha a "scared rabbit" because Martha is quiet.

_____ 4. Joan saw someone shoplifting and reported him to the store manager. Her friends who were with her expressed annoyance at her "sticking her nose in where it didn't belong."

_____ 5. Mary asked Wendy to forgive her for saying something hurtful.

_____ 6. Meg has a group of women at church who side with her on every issue.

_____ 7. Carolyn can be seen praying before each worship service. She asks not to be interrupted.

_____ 8. Madison's son has been addicted to drugs for a year, and she is too ashamed to tell anyone.

_____ 9. Phyllis invites the pastor's family to dinner in her home every week.

_____ 10. Jennifer told a mutual friend that Janet "never made her children behave." Janet was very hurt and decided to talk with Jennifer about it, hoping to prevent her own resentment from growing.

_____ 11. Dell is always immaculately dressed. Her expensive clothes are matched only by the fancy house she lives in.

_____ 12. Jean is adored by many new Christians. She listens to their problems.

Let's examine these. Numbers 1– 3, 6, and 8 are clearly masked behaviors: never admitting mistakes or problems (1, 8), aligning yourself with friends in order to gain power (2, 6), and name-calling to elevate yourself as you belittle others (3), are common behaviors of insecure people. Most of us have engaged in these tactics from time to time.

The numbers 7, 9, 11, and 12 may or may not be masked behaviors.

Carolyn (7) may be protecting her "godly-lady" image by making herself seen praying each Sunday. On the other hand, she may be sincere. Phyllis (9) may be inviting the pastor's family over because they need friends; on the other hand, she may wish to align herself with persons of influence. Dell (11) may mask herself with an outer facade to be admired by others because she needs to portray the best image in order to feel okay about herself. On the other hand, she may be comfortable with nice possessions. How she connects with others may reveal more about the real Dell. Jean (12) may need to be needed. Or she may have the gift of mercy, sincerely caring for others and enjoying counseling.

The numbers 4, 5, and 10 are behaviors of a person who is serious about being real. Mary (5) has removed the mask and humbled herself to ask forgiveness. Janet (10) was honest when she confronted someone who had hurt her. She did not ignore the rift and hope it would go away; she decided to speak the truth in love. Joan (4), experienced the cost of being real: sometimes others do not approve.

HELP! MY HALO IS FALLING!

In order to protect our saintly reputations, even we who are dedicated Christians sometimes fake it, pretending to be joyously spiritual, without a care.

Below are listed problems we may try to hide from others and lies we tell to cover up. Place a check by the areas of your life in which you are most tempted to keep your mask on and your halo perfectly balanced.

❏ 1. Doubts I have about God—"Doubting is a lack of faith, and that's sin."

❏ 2. Insecurities about my attractiveness—"I'm not trying to attract men. I can't help it if they notice me."

❏ 3. Fears—"I can handle it. No big deal."

❏ 4. Past failures—"Me? I would never do such a thing!"

❏ 5. Anger—"I'm not angry; the veins in my forehead always stick out like that."

❏ 6. Disappointments—"No, it's okay. When I have problems, I just rejoice in the Lord and move on."

TAKING OFF THE MASK IS HARD (IF BEING REAL WERE EASY, EVERYBODY WOULD BE DOING IT)

Being real demands not only risk, but also humility. Today, we don't admire people with humility; we tend to laud those with creative vision, decisiveness, and a take-charge personality. In the 2 Kings we are told about a man who had to be humbled before he could be healed.

Read 2 Kings 5:1–5 and answer the following questions.

In 2 Kings 5:1, what qualities do you see in Naaman that others might admire?

_____

_____

Look at 2 Kings 5:2–3. Contrast the persona of the "highly regarded" army commander, a "great man" and war hero, with that of the slave girl from Israel.

_____

_____

In verses 4–6, what evidence do you find that Naaman wished to impress Elisha?

_____

He arrived with clattering horses' hooves and chariots declaring his pompous presence. Can you imagine the swirl of dust he kicked up? What credentials do you sometimes use to impress others? (not necessarily an educational degree; it could be something like "I always did it this way...." or, "In my experience....")

_____

_____

_____

_____

Naaman wasn't yet real. Maybe he thought he couldn't afford to be. After all, his position was the only thing protecting him from the stigma of leprosy and living as an outcast for the rest of his life. But if Naaman thought his power and position would influence Elisha, he was wrong. Elisha instructed him, by way of a messenger, to go dip himself in the dirty Jordan water seven times and promised he would be healed if he obeyed.

What do you think Naaman expected from Elisha (v. 11)?

_____

_____

Naaman's expectations were comical. I think he expected Elisha to flail his arms around like a windmill and chant over him.

Describe Naaman's response in your own words (v. 11).

_____

_____

"You've got to be kidding. No way am I going to get in that slimy river. If you think for one minute that a man of my stature would stoop to such a thing, you must have rocks in your turban," is probably a close facsimile.

Read 2 Kings 5:12–14 and write down how Naaman became real.

_____

_____

Dipping himself in the dirty Jordan River was a humbling experience for Naaman. He had to face his leprosy, admit that the puny river in Israel was good enough for him, and trust this foreign prophet, Elisha, to ask his God to heal him. In short, Naaman took off his mask. Without his fancy uniform, polished chariots, and prancing horses, he was just a leper, standing shivering in the river.

Read 2 Kings 5:15. How do we know that Naaman exchanged his mask for the real thing?

_____

The Scripture records that Naaman "stood humbly" before Elisha and acknowledged the one true God.

If the prayer of your heart is to be real and you wish to pursue the subject, you may begin by reading Be Real by Warren W. Wiersbe.

Read the following words as a supplication to the Lord:

> *Lord,*
> > *I want to be real,*
> > > *to know who I am,*
> > > > *Say what I feel,*
> > > > > *really take a stand,*
> > > > > > *Throw off the mask,*
> > > > > > > *no more pretend,*
> > > > > > > > *Lord, I want to be real.*
> > > > > > > > > —© 1986 Tricia Scribner

The Skin Horse was right. Being real doesn't happen all at once; it is a process of becoming. And sometimes it hurts. But isn't it worth it to be completely whole?

──────── **Always Remember, Never Forget** ────────

The problem with wearing a mask to the masquerade party is that you could end up leaving without anyone knowing who you are.

CHAPTER TWELVE
Seeing Through Your Father's Eyes

I remember visiting our state capitol building when I was eight, racing to the top of the granite stairs.

On the top step, the strap on my new blue pocketbook broke and my money spilled out in ten different directions. Two older girls standing near a marble column near me laughed and pointed at the cheap plastic pocketbook. I was so embarrassed I left the coins and ran back down as fast as I could. My father, who had not seen the incident at the top of the stairs, greeted me below with a hug saying, "You looked like a movie star at the top of the stairs."

Even with my broken plastic pocketbook dangling, I looked up at him and smiled! He had restored my confidence and joy. In my father's eyes, I was almost perfect. All I had seen were my own flaws; all he saw was good. God looks at us in a similar way, seeing our hearts and our greatest potential.

PEOPLE LIKE ME
Most of us are comfortable interacting with people who have similar backgrounds as our own.

Describe yourself and lifestyle.

a. Where do you worship?

_____

b. What style of clothes do you most often wear?

_____

c. What is your educational background?

_____

d. Describe your physical self.

_____

e. In your free time what do you like to do?

_____

f. Describe your personality.

_____

g. What accomplishment are you proud of?

_____

_____

h. Describe your home.

_____

_____

_____

If you were to describe a woman who was just the opposite of how you described yourself and your lifestyle, what would she be like?

_____

_____

Your merea will be different from you in many ways. Check the following lifestyle characteristics that would make you feel awkward or intimidate you. (Be honest with yourself.)

- ❑ She and her friends play golf at the country club every Friday.
- ❑ She wears leggings and a t-shirt most of the time.
- ❑ Her everyday attire includes a briefcase.
- ❑ She did not finish high school.
- ❑ She home-schools her children.
- ❑ She is a corporate executive.
- ❑ Her favorite style of music is rap and loud.
- ❑ She lifts her hands while singing choruses.

❑ She has depression and was recently in a hospital psychiatric ward.
❑ She's loud and boisterous.
❑ She tells jokes containing racial slurs.

List some of your own. Complete the following:

I'd feel awkward if she:

_____

_____

A NEW WAY OF LOOKING AT PEOPLE

Now ask yourself, how does Jesus see this woman with the characteristics so different from yours? Luke 19 shares an example of a situation Jesus faced in which He was called to minister to someone very different from Himself.

Read Luke 19:1–3. What was Zacchaeus like? Describe him.

_____

_____

_____

Zacchaeus was a pretty unlovely character. He was a tax collector, a traitor to the Jews, who worked for the Roman government. He was rich because he took extra money for taxes, gave some to the government and pocketed the rest. He wasn't down and out; he was up and out. He was also short. (Since I'm just over 5'2", I wouldn't hold his height against him.)

Read Luke 19:5–10. How did Jesus respond to Zacchaeus?

_____

_____

_____

The Scripture says that Jesus looked at Zacchaeus; few people probably looked him in the eyes. Perhaps he felt too ashamed to look at people. Jesus showed that He valued Zacchaeus by calling him by name. Then Jesus did something unheard of: He asked to visit Zacchaeus's home. The crowd protested Jesus' effort to get up close and personal with a sinner.

MINISTERING TO THE UP AND OUT

Sometimes we find it easier to give unselfishly to someone who is less fortunate than we are—the down and out. A real test of motives occurs when we are asked to minister to someone whose lifestyle, credentials, or wealth surpasses our own.

What if God calls you to mentor someone who is wealthier, more educated, or more influential in certain circles than you are: someone who is up and out?

Describe a person "out of your league" who would be difficult for you to mentor.

_____

_____

_____

Jesus was able to cut through external trappings to view the person beneath.

What will you do to help you see the person beneath the external trappings?

_____

_____

_____

_____

_____

FIRST–NAME BASIS

Jesus treated Zacchaeus with respect by calling him by name. Maybe He said, "Hey, Zacchaeus!" to which the short guy may have said, "They call me Zack." "Okay, Zack. C'mon down. How about dinner at your house?" Can you picture Zack getting his short legs caught in his Armani robe as he clamored out of that tree? People sneered when he walked by, but that day was different. "Today, I'm gonna get a little respect. This prophet is actually coming to my house to eat. I can't believe he's actually coming over to my place!"

Has anyone ever forgotten your name or called you the wrong name? How did that make you feel?

_____

_____

How do you think Jesus' knowing and calling Zacchaeus by his first name made him feel?

_____

_____

My Aunt Alice, a church secretary in Clinton, South Carolina, told me of an experience that showed her the significance of connecting with someone on a first-name basis. She said, "Mrs. Cooper, an older woman well beyond retirement age, offered to help me fold bulletins in the church office. One day she said, 'Alice, you always call me Mrs. Cooper. That makes me feel like an old lady. I want to be your friend. Call me Lena.' From then on, Lena and I were best friends. She was never Mrs. Cooper again."

Every woman prefers being called a name that she feels fits her. Some people have nicknames; others dread being called a nickname. Never shorten someone's name without permission. Tricia, whose given name is Patricia, hates it when people take the liberty of nicknaming her Pat, Patsy, or Patty, not because those names are bad, but they don't fit her. Ask your merea what she wishes to be called, even if others call her by a nickname. Asking shows respect for her preference. Also avoid the use of condescending names such as "hon."

UP CLOSE AND PERSONAL

When Jesus saw Zack up close and personal, He saw all Zack's unlovely traits, but He also saw deeper into his heart. As a mentor, you will ask God to enable you to look beneath the warts!

My husband developed a habit shortly after we married that irritated me to distraction. (Maybe I was so much in love with him that I had never noticed earlier!) Before he drank from a glass, he held it up at eye level, squinted, and sighted the other side of the glass across the surface of the water. The first time he held his glass high, I thought he was going to make a toast; strange behavior for a man who didn't drink alcohol. I asked him what he was doing. Was the glass dirty? Had I left lipstick on the rim? Or was he just crazy? He explained that as a child he liked movies about submarines with periscopes coming out of the water, and a glass reminded him of that childhood memory. Week after week I ate meals with the periscope man, squinting and drinking, and I became more irritated day after day.

One night he was late for dinner, and I missed the periscope sightings as I ate alone. I realized I had grown to love even this eccentric behavior. When he came in four hours later, shaken up from an accident, I smiled as he picked up his glass, lifted it high, squinted to analyze the surface of the water, and then drank his iced tea. "God love him," I thought. "He is wonderful."

As you grow closer to your merea, you will find her background, traditions, and lifestyle may be different from your own. May God grant you the patience to love even her quirks up close and personal.

List some traits of your merea (or a dear friend if you don't know your merea yet) which challenge your patience and understanding.

_____

_____

_____

SEEING EYE-TO-EYE

Tricia learned the hard way how subtly a condescending attitude can creep in and damage a relationship. "When I was a public health nurse responsible for home health care, I went to a home where Donna, a single mom, cared for a bedridden relative along with her own three children. The house was cramped, with no air conditioning in the humid, 90-degree heat. As usual, I started looking at the patient, assessing her needs and problems. Marcie, the relative, lay on a bed, contorted from a stroke, barely able to move, and unable to speak. The bedsheets were wadded, the room reeked of urine, and Marcie's body odor was bad enough to make me back up. I began to straighten the area and ask Donna how she cared for Marcie. The more questions I asked, the shorter Donna's answers became. Finally she walked out of the room. I followed, sat beside her on the couch, and asked what was wrong.

"'It seems like you don't think I'm doing a very good job,' she said.

"I realized I had come across as though I were looking down on her in my brisk assessment of the patient's condition. Looking her in the eye, I said, 'It must be hard to be a single mom, take care of your three children, and take care of all of Marcie's needs, too. What you are doing is amazing. I can't imagine how you do all this-making beds, giving medicine, playing with the children, preparing meals, feeding Marcie as well as your kids.' She cried. From that day on, we were close friends because she knew I respected her."

Jesus didn't show Zacchaeus deference because of his wealth. Neither did He look down on Zacchaeus because of his evil heart. Instead, He went to Zacchaeus's home, and reclining at the supper table as was customary at that time, looked at Zacchaeus eye-to-eye.

Read the examples and verses. How will viewing your merea through your Father's eyes affect your response in the following situations?

1. When I feel angry at her immature ways: Matthew 7:1–5.

_____

_____

2. When she doesn't seem to understand what I'm trying to teach her: Job 29:15.

_____

_____

3. When she does something that embarrasses me: 1 Thessalonians 5:14–15.

_____

_____

4. When she has more than I do, in terms of wealth, education, etc.: 1 Corinthians 13:4.

_____

_____

5. When I feel free to do something that might cause my merea to stumble:1 Corinthians 8:9.

_____

_____

Your place of service as a mentor is not above your merea, looking down from your lofty spiritual position. It is not looking up, intimidated by her wealth or prestige. Your place is directly across from her. Look her straight in the eye just as Jesus did Zack. You can do it if you see her through your Father's eyes.

——— Always Remember, Never Forget ———

We are all the same height at the supper table.

CHAPTER THIRTEEN
Developing Heart-Core Intimacy

Some memories print themselves indelibly in your mind and heart forever.

My husband's death was one of those. I'll never forget that October night when we went nonchalantly to our local high school football game and I came home a widow. I'll always remember his soft voice as he collapsed on the stadium seat with a heart attack, the look of his eyes as they rolled back—all white; the rush of the crowd to give CPR, the loud speaker blaring, "Is there a doctor in the stands?" and the ambulance with our family doctor leaning over my dying husband trying to resuscitate him, but to no avail.

Mostly I remember the lonely months that followed. Our son Jack was in college, so only sixteen-year-old Patsy and I remained at home. My bed seemed so lonely that I slept with her many nights. We went to movies, ate pizza, and just drove around town to keep busy. Previous mother/daughter friction faded as we prayed for each other, supported each other in grief, and clung to each other, deepening our bond.

Now that Patsy is an adult, I sometimes think about how we became so close. I remember the countless shared traditions and experiences, even painful ones, such as the loss of her father, that drove our relationship into heart-core intimacy.

Do you hope for this level of intimacy with your merea?

❑ definitely
❑ I haven't really thought about it

Heart-core intimacy develops in a relationship when each person translates shared traditions, shared experiences, shared humor, and each person's uniqueness into meaning, not only for the individual, but also for the pair.

THE BOND OF COMMON GROUND
In the initial phases of a relationship, discussions tend to gravitate toward areas of common ground. You and your merea can look for things you have in

common to help you to begin bonding with each other.

1. Life Traditions

Traditions such as unique dress, food preferences, and religious customs provide a common ground that binds cultural groups into close-knit communities. The experience of Walker, one of Patsy's friends, shows the significance of traditions. When he attended Columbia University, a few classmates invited him to attend a lecture by a famous speaker. The speaker referred to Jesus' illustrations of the lost sheep and the widow's mite.

As they drove back to the campus, one student said, "That was the worst speech I've ever heard. Nothing made sense; he just rambled on and on."

Another student agreed. "It was terrible," he said. "The ninety and nine...What is that? Something to do with sheep."

A third spoke up: "And I didn't like the story about that woman's bug."

Ted, the student sitting beside Walker, said, "Wait a minute. Haven't you ever heard of the widow's mite? That's a coin, not a bug! It was a masterful speech: three main points followed by clear illustrations and the best ending I've ever heard."

Then Walker realized the difference in perspectives: he and Ted were Christians whose traditions included the telling of New Testament stories; the others were Jews whose traditions included stories only from the Old Testament. Walker and Ted were connected by a tradition they had in common.

Read Luke 15:3–7. Why do you think Jesus used the illustration of a lost sheep to portray God's love for every person?

_____

_____

_____

Jesus used illustrations with which the people were familiar. Although Walker's friends were unfamiliar with the custom of herding sheep, the group to whom Jesus spoke immediately understood Jesus' example since it was a part of their everyday lives.

2. Life Experiences

Tricia is a preacher's kid. She says that during her teen years she often felt isolated because of the demands placed upon her. No one seemed to understand the stresses of living in a pastor's family. A few years ago she served as a counselor for a retreat where all the staff and teens were also preachers' kids. She says, "For the first time in my life I worshiped in a room full of people like me: people who could understand my struggles as a PK. I immediately felt connected with them."

Check the following life experiences you have in common with a friend or your merea; if the person you chose is not your merea, in the blank beside write the name or initials of the person with whom you have that experience in common.

- ❏ Serious illness _____
- ❏ Parents divorced _____
- ❏ Death of a close loved one _____
- ❏ Marriage _____
- ❏ Profession _____
- ❏ Rearing children _____
- ❏ Frequent moves _____
- ❏ Singleness _____

Can you think of other significant personal experiences that bind you to another person? Describe them below.

_____

_____

_____

_____

_____

_____

3. Spiritual Experiences

In her book *A Garden Path to Mentoring*, Esther Burroughs writes an insightful description of Jesus' mother, Mary, and her cousin, Elizabeth, from Luke 1. (You will want to read her poignant portrayal of this pair in her book, pp. 7–10.) These Jewish women enjoyed not only shared tradition, which Mary recounts in Mary's Song, sometimes called the Magnificat—Luke 1:46–55, but also spiritual experience and understanding. For example, they both experienced supernatural visits from angels.

Read Luke 1:11–25 and 26–38. Describe ways in which Mary's and Elizabeth's spiritual experiences were similar.

Luke 1:11–25	Luke 1:26–38
_____	_____
_____	_____
_____	_____

Burroughs says, "Mary and Elizabeth shared the language of the heart. But they went further—they shared the language and feeling of God's heart. Spiritual depth is the foundation for Christian mentoring!"

Check the following spiritual experiences which you have in common with someone else; in the blank jot down the name of a person with whom you have that experience in common.

- ❏ Salvation _____
- ❏ Baptism _____
- ❏ Marriage _____
- ❏ Personal restoration/healing _____
- ❏ Joy in worship _____
- ❏ Lord's Supper (Eucharist) _____
- ❏ Commitment to serving in church_____
- ❏ Christian parents/upbringing _____
- ❏ Area of ministry _____
- ❏ Love of missions _____
- ❏ Giftedness _____
- ❏ Other: _____

THE BOND OF SHARED EVENTS

I once went on an overnight prayer retreat with Andrea Mullins, a Christian friend and coworker. Since we both love Psalm 139, I was delighted to learn she had memorized it as a gift for me. She presented it to me as we walked and prayed, reciting it word for word. Even now, I think of her every time I read Psalm 139.

1. Making Memories

Mary and Elizabeth were both pregnant at the same time. What a bond they had! Perhaps you were pregnant at the same time as a cousin or a neighbor. This gave you instant rapport. Even if it was not at the same time, giving birth seems to bond all mothers. (If you don't believe it, just mention your delivery-hour experiences in a room full of women and see how many of them share theirhorror stories!)

Which of the following do you share with your merea or a close friend?

We like to:

- ❏ go on missions trips
- ❏ shop till we drop
- ❏ exercise
- ❏ share our problems and pray

❑ eat out at a favorite restaurant (or any restaurant!)
❑ share a hobby: _____

Patsy, my daughter, often reminds me, when our plans for fun turn chaotic, "Remember, we're not trying to accomplish anything here, we're just making memories." Build a storehouse of memories by enjoying everyday experiences together with your merea.

2. Shared Humor

Sometimes called an inside joke, moments of humor can cement a relationship and draw a twosome closer. You may hear someone say, "You had to be there" to indicate the intimacy of shared humor. A shared belly laugh adds much to a relationship.

A former merea in California calls me occasionally and says, "Sniglet," which sends me into rollicking laughter because of a workshop we attended which used sniglets, or "fractured words." These are two favorites:

Pencilventilation:	The act of sharpening your pencil and then blowing on it.
Aquadextrous:	Being able to sit in a bathtub and turn on the water with your toes.

Tricia and her mom shared a humorous, although painful, bonding experience one evening when they went to a health club together. After finishing the exercise class, Tricia realized they were almost late for Wednesday night prayer meeting. Hurriedly, she sat down to put on her street shoes. When she stood and turned to walk out, she smacked her head into a barbell poised on a rack. Smarting from the pain and embarrassment, she rushed out the door, only to hear a loud clunk inside. Her mom came out the door rubbing her head. Not only had she run into the same barbell, but the impact had knocked it to the floor! Tricia said that now when people say, "You are a lot like your mother," she and her mom look at each other and laugh, thinking, *If they only knew.*

Can you recall a word, phrase, or memory that triggers laughter between you and another person? Share it here.

_____

_____

_____

3. Celebrating Uniqueness

Not only can having traditions in common and making memories together bind you and your merea, but also recognizing differences can cement your relationship. Your merea is unique and so are you. As your mentoring relationship deepens, you each will find joy in your uniqueness. Tricia and I, as writing mentor and merea, are polarized opposites, but each of us celebrates—and yes, even loves—the uniqueness (and the challenges) of the other. We complement each other in the most amazing ways.

Tricia tends to analyze her writing meticulously, while I just go with the flow. One weekend Tricia and I met in San Jose, California, to work on this book. As I curled up in a pillowed corner of the room with my old legal pad, Tricia sat at the desk. She leaned back from the computer and reflected: "I've been looking at my writing, wondering. . . is it just fluff—a string of eloquent words for the sake of language? Or is it honest, a flow straight from God that reflects the innermost part of me?"

"Oh, shucks, Tricia," I said. "I never think like that at all. Before I begin writing, I ask God to let me say something He'll like and then I write down whatever comes out. I trust it—whatever it is—and then say, 'Bless this mess, Lord,' when I'm finished."

As well as enjoying shared experiences and traditions you and your merea may have in common, celebrate each of your unique attributes, even those that show differences in the way you approach life. If you and your merea do not have much in common, particularly if she is not a Christian or comes from a completely different background than you, begin to build your own storehouse of memories you can later reminisce about.

Tricia and I have made so many memories! Rehashing them is like tying a pretty bow around a treasured gift and tucking it in a tender place in my heart forever. Whenever you share experiences with your merea, you, too, are making memories you both will revisit together.

———— Always Remember, Never Forget ————

If you can't share sniglets or bumping barbells,
at least eat a Twinkie together.

CHAPTER FOURTEEN
Building Trust Through Accountability and Confidentialit

What does it mean to be accountable? Webster's says to be accountable means to be "answerable" or "responsible."

ACCOUNTABILITY

Each person is accountable to God. This means that you are responsible to or answerable to Him for your actions and attitudes. A child must be mature enough to understand that she, and she alone, is answerable to God for her behavior, her sin, and most importantly, for her acceptance or rejection of Christ as the only way to salvation. Christians often call the age at which a child reaches this point of understanding "the age of accountability."

Sometimes we confuse being responsible to and being responsible for someone. When it comes to salvation, for instance, you are responsible to your children for rearing them in such a way that they are continually exposed to the truths and the ways of God. But whether your children respond to God's invitation for salvation is their decision. You are not responsible for their salvation; each person is responsible to God individually.

In your mentoring relationship, you and your merea are responsible to each other.

Write down issues for which you and your merea are answerable to each other.

_____

_____

_____

You are answerable to each other about issues such as keeping planned meetings, being on time, keeping personal matters in confidence, preparing ahead of time for studies you may do together, praying for each other, honoring each other's time constraints, and generally keeping promises.

Since you both are answerable to each other about issues affecting your mentoring relationship, if you or your merea fails to keep a promise, talk about it. Clarify your expectations, and if you are the one who failed, model for her how to ask forgiveness and set the relationship back on course.

CONFIDENTIALITY

Your merea has confided in you information which makes you very uncomfortable. You are not sure how to handle the situation. Check beside the principle which will most guide your decision whether to talk to someone and if so, whom and how.

1. ❏   I think it is best never to promise confidentiality; that way I'm not bound by a promise I can't keep.

2. ❏   Under no circumstances would I share personal information gleaned from a private conversation with my merea.

3. ❏   I would not disclose information shared in the mentoring relationship unless there were a specific moral obligation to do so.

4. ❏   In order to mentor wisely I will need the freedom to ask for guidance from others I trust, such as my prayer partner, the mentor support team, or pastoral staff. There may be times I will share private information.

If you had trouble choosing only one or any of the responses, then you understand something of the complexity of confidentiality issues. A nugget of truth can be identified in each statement. A blanket promise of confidentiality could get you into trouble if a problem arises in which you need to consult someone else.

In a nonprofessional setting, a person who asks about confidentiality is usually requesting privacy. The goal of assuring privacy is twofold: 1) to show respect to the person by keeping personal information and conversation private, and 2) to lay the foundation for trust.

DEALING WITH ISSUES OF PRIVACY

Every person has a right to have personal feelings, thoughts, and actions kept from general public knowledge. Only your merea has the right to share her own personal experiences with others. Be aware that privacy does not only pertain to issues of a potentially hurtful nature, but also to everyday incidents, as well as her personal view of life. Let her speak for herself.

Privacy is privacy only when both parties agree to the same guidelines at the onset of the relationship. The mentor needs assurance of privacy as much as the merea. As a mentor, you may disclose information or personal experience in casual conversation or in an effort to minister to your merea's needs.

You can share openly only if you trust your merea to honor your privacy.

Your merea may share information with you that you feel is beyond your ability to handle or that you feel a moral obligation to disclose. Usually, these are issues of safety for herself or others. At the beginning of your relationship, discuss how you will deal with this possibility. You may assure your merea that if you need to consult someone or even ask for prayer about a personal problem she has confided in you, you will discuss your plan with her and that she will be part of the process.

One way to deal with the issue of privacy is to write out and sign a statement of understanding and agreement as part of your mentor/merea covenant. Open communication at the beginning of the relationship is the best way to prevent misunderstanding, hurt, and broken trust.

THIS MATTER OF TRUST

Since developing trust is so important for you and your merea, take a closer look at this word.

What does it mean to trust someone?

_____

_____

When you trust someone, you place yourself in that person's care, leaning hard on that person's dependable, loyal character.

Think of people in your life whom you most trust. What character traits make them people in whom you can place confidence?

_____

_____

_____

_____

_____

I would trust a mentor who would not laugh with others about my silliness, or talk about the kinks in my personality, or roll her eyes to someone when my name was mentioned. I would trust a mentor, who, if she needed to consult someone about a personal problem I had shared with her, would talk with me about it first. I would trust a mentor who did not need to impress others with knowing inside information about me.

Read Proverbs 25:19. The Amplified Bible says it like this: "Confidence in

an unfaithful man in time of trouble is like a broken tooth or a foot out of joint." Write the verse as it is written in your Bible translation.

_____

_____

_____

_____

List actions you will take to guard yourself from dishonoring your merea's trust.

_____

_____

_____

_____

COVENANT FRIENDSHIP

The mentor/merea relationship is a covenant friendship; that is, the friendship is founded on commitment to one another's good and is sealed with an agreement between friends. Jonathan and David illustrate the most endearing covenant friendship described in the Scriptures.

Read 1 Samuel 20:12–42 and answer the questions.

First Samuel 20:12–17—Jonathan knew David would become king instead of himself. How did Jonathan respond?

_____

_____

First Samuel 20:19–23, 35–37—How did Jonathan demonstrate his commitment to keep promises?

_____

_____

First Samuel 20:39—How did Jonathan show his ability to keep a confidence?

_____

_____

Jonathan demonstrated character traits worthy of trust. Although Jonathan realized that David one day would take the throne that was Jonathan's by lawful right, Jonathan was not jealous; in fact, he prayed God would bless David as king (v. 13). He promised that he would go to find out Saul's attitude toward David, and then would return and inform David. He kept his promise (v. 35). Jonathan then gave the signal to alert David that Saul intended to kill him so that David could flee for safety. Verse 39 makes it clear that the young boy with Jonathan knew nothing about the signal Jonathan and David had designed. Jonathan kept David's location to himself and saved David's life.

The Relationship Between Trust and Your Merea's Spiritual Growth

The visual below shows why safety and trust within the mentor/merea relationship are foundational for the merea's healing and spiritual growth.

Starting on the left at Step 1, read upward to Step 4 on the far right.

Leaning to Learning: Steps of a Merea's Growth

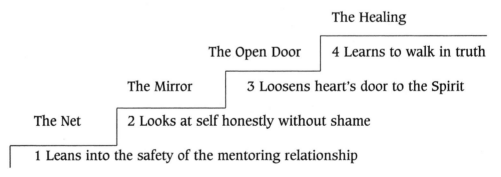

The Healing

The Open Door | 4 Learns to walk in truth

The Mirror | 3 Loosens heart's door to the Spirit

The Net | 2 Looks at self honestly without shame

1 Leans into the safety of the mentoring relationship

In step one, as the mentor lays the foundation for trust, the merea leans into the safety net of the relationship. In step two, the merea looks in the mirror at herself more honestly, able to acknowledge her struggles because she fears no shaming from within the relationship. In step three, the merea loosens her heart's door to the convicting, correcting, and comforting power of the Holy Spirit. In step four, she learns and applies truth to her life. Like the paralyzed man whom Jesus healed (Matt. 9:6), she, too, takes up her mat and walks in healing.

Looking at the Leaning to Learning visual, in which step do you see the mentor playing the most active role? (circle one) Step: 1   2   3   4

The mentor plays a critical role in providing a safety net (Step 1) for the merea—a place she can fall without breaking. Remember, trust grows in relation to the safety your merea experiences within your relationship. While other variables beyond your control will affect your merea's ability to feel safe and to trust, your respecting her privacy and keeping promises will go a long way toward mending old hurts. If she can count on your word and feels free to be transparent with you—free to share sins, worries, and failures without fear of judgment—you will enable her to open her heart to the work of the Holy Spirit and live in the truth He reveals.

Go back and review Proverbs 25:19 from the Amplified Bible version, earlier in this study. Complete the verse.

"Confidence in an unfaithful man in time of trouble is like a broken _____ or a foot out of _____."

―――――― **Always Remember, Never Forget** ――――――

Avoid broken teeth and disjointed feet
by keeping promises and honoring privacy.

CHAPTER FIFTEEN
The How and Why of Boundaries

She's called three times this week for a ride.

Today, Tonie, your merea, says her car is still in the shop and asks you to take her to the grocery store at 4:30 this afternoon. You are free at that time, but were looking forward to some quiet time. You feel resentful that she has called so much lately.

Circle any item that reflects how you might respond to her request.

    a. Say "yes" since I don't have a good excuse.

    b. Say "no" and feel very guilty.

    c. Say "no" and give a very long explanation of all I have to do.

    d. Say "yes" and ask God to forgive me for feeling resentful.

If you circled any of the above, you may have problems setting boundaries.

ABOUT FENCES AND NEIGHBORS

Robert Frost, in his poem, *Mending Wall*, described two neighbors mending the barrier that separated their property. One was inclined to leave it broken, pointing out to his neighbor that since only trees were growing there, they were not likely to infringe on the other's property, and the wall could be left as it was. The other neighbor continued mending and responded, "Good fences make good neighbors."

The wary neighbor was right in that the physical boundaries of our home such as walls, doors, fences, and property lines tell us what is and is not our responsibility to care for. Those boundaries also free us to do with our property as we wish. I appreciated this truth much more after losing that freedom.

In Louisiana, we lived in a rural area with a huge yard and flower beds. I hated weeding around the azaleas, and I also hated the eternal (or was that infernal?) mowing. Then our family of five moved into a two-bedroom apartment with no yard. No grass to mow—no weeds to pick. Should've been heaven, right? Wrong. No grass to mow meant no place to hide Easter eggs. No weeds meant no fragrant flowers. I missed the smell of honeysuckle in bloom. I missed the pine needles falling on my deck. I missed green.

Two houses later, I've decided that while I may hate gardening, I love growing things. I plant on every bare spot of dirt. I get excited about planting because it's my garden, and when the tomatoes are ready I can pick as many as I want and eat them until I'm sick. The joy would be lost if I were not sure where our property line fell. What if I had accidentally planted the tomatoes on my neighbor's property? Devastating. Knowing your boundaries is really important.

WHAT IS A BOUNDARY?

A boundary, then, is an internal "property line" that lets you know what is and is not your responsibility. Boundaries are evident in all arenas of our lives: physical, emotional, mental, and spiritual.

- **Physical Boundaries**
  Have you ever felt awkward when someone talked in your face too closely? Your internal physical boundary line informed you that your personal space was being invaded. You may have taken a step back trying to regain your comfort zone.

What physical boundaries have you set for yourself or taught your children?

_____

_____

- **Mental Boundaries**
  Your thoughts and opinions are unique and separate from anyone else's. My father was a military man, then a pastor. The rules were the rules, and personal opinion had little opportunity to rear its ugly head. As an adult, I struggled knowing whether my opinions were truly my own beliefs or whether I was just parroting old things from childhood. Making decisions was very difficult. Later in counseling, as I began to view myself as a separate human being, I became more able to trust my own decisions.

List two opinions you hold as an adult which are different from those of your parents.

_____

- **Emotional Boundaries**

  Emotional boundaries allow you to acknowledge your feelings without shame or self-blame. They help you take in what is good and keep the bad out so it doesn't harm your inner identity.

  Years ago, when someone criticized me, I assumed that the person's criticism was true. While externally I responded defensively, inwardly I kicked myself for not being able to do anything right. I felt great shame. Now, more often I can take in any valuable truth from the criticism and discard the rest, while knowing I am worthy with or without the perceived or actual failure.

Recall a time someone criticized you. How did you feel about yourself during that experience?

_____

_____

- **Spiritual Boundaries**

  Spiritual boundaries allow you to experience God as a separate person, who cherishes you and wants to live in and guide you, but who will not invade where you have not invited.

Read Revelation 3:20. Write the verse below.

_____

_____

_____

That God respects your boundaries is the essence of free will. Think of it. God Almighty humbles Himself and waits at your heart's door until you grant permission for Him to enter.

Does God Have Boundaries?

To say that God honors your boundaries does not mean that God does not have His own boundaries. On the contrary, He sets the best example of how boundaries work.

Read Genesis 2:16–17. Describe the boundary God placed for Adam and Eve.

_____

_____

Read Genesis 3:23–24. What happened when Adam and Eve dishonored God's boundary line?

_____

_____

God granted permission for Adam and Eve to eat fruit of any tree in the garden except one—the tree of the knowledge of good and evil. When they disobeyed and dishonored God's boundary, He enforced the promised consequences: He forced them to leave the garden.

LIMIT-SETTING AS A LOVING ACTION

Our family had gone to the movies and out to eat—and eat and eat. The children had consumed enough food to go into hibernation and live off the storage. Arriving home, our 10-year-old, Sara, complained of her stomach hurting, then asked for a milkshake. We said, "No way." Saying "yes" not only would have been unhealthy for her, it also would have indulged her whims without meeting her true need: to set boundaries on herself that are ultimately in her best interest. Children need boundaries in order to learn how to set healthy boundaries in their own lives. So do grown-ups.

Read Genesis 3:22. How did God's sending Adam and Eve out of the garden demonstrate His love?

_____

_____

God showed His love by being true to His Word: He was trustworthy. Also some scholars believe that had the tree of knowledge of good and evil sustained physical life in man's sinful state, the misery would have been intolerable.

LIES THAT TAKE YOU IN AND BURN YOU OUT

Consider how harried we feel when we are overextended. What conditions could possibly make us disregard our internal boundaries and say "yes" when we want to say "no"?

1. **"The Need Is the Call"**
    Between us, my husband and I held a total of 12 positions in our local church. The need was great. But I was exhausted. The joy of service had been sapped out of me, leaving only grudging obedience. Need alone can't define your ministry because the need will always be bigger than you.

Read John 12:3–8. How did Christ respond to Judas?

_____

_____

Jesus received the anointing, even though selling the perfume could have bought bread for someone starving. He affirmed the significance of her anointing as preparation for His death—the death by which every person could receive eternal life.

Let the Lord's call and the desire of your heart define your ministry. Any other service is just tinkling brass.

2. **"I'm Qualified Therefore I Should"**
   The fact that you are *able* to do something does not mean that you *should* do it. A friend of mine was great with kids. She worked with the children's choir. Problem was, she hated it. Children drove her nuts although she loved them. She felt obligated because she was able to perform well. A second twist to this idea is that if you are asked to serve, and you have the time, then you should do it. I agree with Dr. Richard Swenson, who, in his book *Margin*, suggests that most of us live with our emotional energy accounts overdrawn, leaving less time for meditation and relationships. Without anything in reserve, you have little to give.

List jobs you have taken on just because you were qualified to do them.

_____

_____

3. **"I'm Not a Good Mentor Unless I Am Available When My Merea Needs Me"**
   Kim had mentored Leslie for several months. Leslie called several times a week, "just to talk." Kim noticed that the calls were lasting longer and longer, interfering with the time she usually spent helping her children with homework. She decided to screen her calls and return them at a more convenient time. When she told Leslie, Leslie said, "I thought when you became my mentor that meant you would be there for me. How can I get your support and guidance if I can't reach you when I need you?"

What would your gut-level reaction be in this situation?

_____

———————————————————

———————————————————

———————————————————

RESPONDING TO THE DEMANDS OF OTHERS

How would you respond to Leslie's comment? If you would feel resentful, guilty, or defensive, then you may find the following techniques helpful, adapted from the book, *Boundaries* by Dr. Henry Cloud and Dr. John Townsend.

1. Recognize the guilt-provoking comment as thinly disguised anger. Do notengage in explanation or self-defense. You do not need to explain why you made your decision or why you were not available.

2. Assertively interpret the message as being about her feelings. "It sounds to me like you are hurt that I was not available to answer your call."

3. Reassert your boundary. "You are right, I won't always be available."

4. Empathize with her. "I can tell that this is hard for you."

5. Reaffirm your care and commitment. "Our relationship is important to me. I do have 15 minutes now (*if you do*). Could we use this time to talk?"

Integrating boundaries into your life is not easy, but the efforts you make at placing appropriate boundaries around yourself and your time will yield more energy to serve, as well as give you more peace. Sometimes others will not understand your purpose in saying no. So get the support you need. Reading *Boundaries* is a great start.

——————— **Always Remember, Never Forget** ———————

Boundary in or burn out!

CHAPTER SIXTEEN
Keeping Your Well Full

As a young housewife, I didn't know how to say no to anyone who asked me to serve.

NO TIME FOR REFILLS

Just as Tricia shared in the previous chapter, I, too, was overcommitted. I baked pies for church socials, wrote poetry for a Christian coffee shop owner to display, painted watercolors with poor children, taught an adult Sunday school class, led the women's missions organization at our church, took sermon tapes to shut-ins, and provided three meals a day and an almost-clean house for two children and a husband. When I finally sat down for my quiet time with the Lord, I often nodded off just after "Dear Lord." (Can't you hear Him saying, "There goes Edna again, face down in Jeremiah 5!")

One day I realized I was so busy doing His work that I didn't have time for Him. My well was dry.

FILL IT UP, PLEASE

God never intends for you to be depleted or dry of spirit. Pursuing your own spiritual growth in the Lord is the most important preparation for your mentoring. The mentoring you do grows from an overflow of the Living Water coming from your spiritual well.

If you are one who feels guilty when you think of meeting your own needs first, remember what flight attendants advise those passengers traveling with small children to do in an emergency: "Put on your own oxygen mask first; then place the oxygen mask on your child."

Read Proverbs 4:23. Why is it so important that you "watch over your heart" (NASB)?

_____

_____

Read Matthew 12:34–35. How do you think your own spiritual condition will affect the way you speak to your merea?

_____

_____

LIVING WATER

The most vivid picture of Christ as the Living Water is found in the story of Jesus and the Samaritan woman at Jacob's well.

Read John 4:5–14. The woman spoke of physical water while Jesus spoke of _____ water. In the list below, how would you match the characteristics of physical water in the left column with spiritual water in the right column?

Physical		**Spiritual**
_____ 1. Refreshes	a.	He fulfills a yearning for righteousness
_____ 2. Quenches thirst	b.	He energizes
_____ 3. Soothes a burning throat	c.	He makes whole; restores
_____ 4. Heals by rehydrating	d.	He overcomes the pain of sin

(Just for fun, see if you matched the above as I did: 1–b; 2–a; 3–d; 4–c)

FLOWING WATER

Imagine you are standing by a freshwater stream. You look back and notice that down the hill is a stagnant pond. Using all your senses, describe the differences in how you experience the two.

_____

_____

When I picture myself in that setting, I'm reluctant to walk near the stagnant pond. It stinks. Green scum coats the water surface. The thought of drinking it makes me sick, and I fear what lurks beneath the murky water. On the other hand, the freshwater stream is so clear I can see tiny fish flitting about on the bottom. The water gurgles and splashes across the rocks; the smell is clean; the water feels cold to my mouth and tastes almost sweet; the stream invites me to take off my shoes, stick my toes in, and stay a while.

Read John 4:11 and John 4:14.

These two verses make a similar comparison between the well the woman described and the spiritual well Jesus was speaking of. Two different Greek words are used for the word *well* in these two verses. The woman wanted the living water, but thought it must be drawn from the physical well, a *phrear* (FREH-ar), or pit dug in the earth to hold water. She was worried because Jesus had nothing with which to pull out the water. Jesus responded to her, knowing that the person who drinks from Him does not need to reach down for the water with a bucket. Instead, from within will spring up a *pege* (pay-GAY), a well or fountain of bubbling, surging, gushing, living water.

To review, fill in the blanks below:

A _____ describes a pit dug in the earth that holds water.

A _____ describes a well or fountain of bubbling, surging, living water.

How would you describe your heart, as a phrear or a pege? The truth is, if Jesus Christ lives within, your heart is a pege. If you don't feel like a pege, that's okay. Sometimes we don't tap into our greatest source of strength because we don't know how.

Tricia shared an incident that illustrates this point. Her microwave was sick. It scorched popcorn, while leaving a jillion (her word) kernels in the bottom of the bag. Over the weeks she tried everything she knew to fix the problem: repositioning the bag, altering the cooking time, and making sure the right side of the bag was facing up. Eventually she gave up and called the repair man. He walked in the front door, took one look at the microwave and said, "Do you have a glass pan?" She passed him one and stood with a stricken look on her face as he turned it upside down, placed it in the microwave, and said, "That oughta' fix your problem. The food needs to be raised so it can cook from all sides." He left no more than three minutes after he had walked in the door, right after he charged her $67.00 for the visit.

"What bugged me the most," Tricia said, "was that I had everything I needed to fix the problem right there in my house. I just didn't know how to use it."

OPENING THE FLOW

You may think that you have little time to pray, study God's Word, or begin new spiritual development now that you are setting aside extra time to mentor someone. Even so, you may routinely engage in activities that will help keep your well full.

Which of the following do you participate in often? Circle all that apply:

Daily Bible reading	Prayer meeting/group	Church worship
Small-group Bible study	Reading a Christian growth book	Discipleship group
Memorizing Scriptures	Meditation during long walks	Meeting with your own mentor
Prayer with a friend	Physical fitness/exercise	
Alone time with God	Accountability times with a friend	

One activity worth your time investment is developing a prayer support system. Surround yourself with pray-ers who will love you and your merea enough to intentionally pray for both of you. Earnest prayer of righteous persons who agree together is like turning the spigot of your water faucet to the "on" position. Prayer enables the underwater spring of the Holy Spirit to flow up through you and overflow into the life of your merea. Don't be surprised if you see your merea growing by leaps and bounds (as well as yourself) when you have earnestly sought out true prayer warriors to support you.

Name a special prayer partner you will ask to covenant with you to pray:

_____

Name a second person who will covenant to pray:

_____

Name a third person who will covenant to pray:

_____

Three persons joined together to pray for a certain situation form a prayer triplet. If you are mentoring within an organized women's ministry, you may have a mentor support team, consisting of several members praying for you regularly. Either way, prayer support is not a luxury; it is a necessity.

Check the following areas of your life in which you most need prayer support at this time:

- ❑ Godliness in my daily walk
- ❑ Healthy relationship between me and my spouse
- ❑ Healthy relationship between me and my children
- ❑ Physical health
- ❑ Emotional health and stability

❑ Stamina
❑ Protection against the interference of Satan
❑ Ability to speak boldly
❑ Release from the need to perform well to feel good
❑ Other (describe):

A MATTER OF IMPORTANCE

First Chronicles 28 tells the story of the Hebrews rebuilding the temple. King David instructed his son Solomon to place priorities on each object used in worship. He assigned certain values to each candlestick, vase, and decoration (vv. 10–18), then added embellishments according to the value of each. The highest value was assigned to the object that represented the seat of God's presence: the Ark of the Covenant.

Read 1 Corinthians 6:19–20. Where is now the seat of God's presence?

_____

_____

_____

How does knowing that you are now the sanctuary of God's presence, His favorite dwelling place, affect you right now?

_____

_____

_____

Keep My Well Full of Water

Help me, Father, when I'm busy
Always rushing to and fro.
Take me to the heart of God
Where the streams of water flow.

Slow me down enough to drink
The healing water for my soul;
Living water, fresh ideas,
Hydro power and energy roll.

My source is You, Almighty Father;
May I come to You each day,
Take delight in all You tell me,
In Your presence splash and play.

May I listen to You, Father
Hands uplifted, Your dear daughter
Reaching, catching, overflowing;
You keep my well full of water.

—© 1998 Edna Ellison

Dear Mentor, guard your own lifeline to God so you will be able to offer the water of life to another. As you mentor, you will find every minute is precious. God knows your sacrifice as you rearrange schedules, ask your family for understanding, and practice all the time management principles you have learned from experience over the years. He will guide you. But remember: stay close to Him.

─────── **Always Remember, Never Forget** ───────

A *pege* is better than a *phrear* because moving water doesn't collect bugs.

CHAPTER SEVENTEEN
Age Difference Makes a Difference

The difference in years between the mentor and merea has a significant impact on the dynamics of the relationship.

Just ask Edna. At fifteen, Edna met a young man and fell in love. She wanted to marry him after she finished high school. Only one thing stood in the way: her parents. Like most parents, they saw their daughter as a child. One night her family visited relatives. After dinner her cousin Shirley, who was five years older, cleared the table and began washing dishes. When Edna asked Shirley to leave the dishes and come have fun, her cousin responded, "Are you crazy? My mother's not going to let me get married if I'm lazy. I try to act like an adult every chance I get."

Her words fell on eager ears and from that moment on, Edna says she cleared the table at mealtime, washed dishes, stored them, and even prepared meals anytime her mother was away or busy. Later, she modeled herself after Shirley in other ways, asking for advice on dating, cooking, and housekeeping.

In the story above, what do you see as some of the benefits of having a mentor who is about five years older than you?

_____

_____

What drawbacks could there be to having a mentor who is *only* five years older than you?

_____

_____

Mentor/merea pairs who are separated in age by 5 years interact differently than pairs whose age difference spans 30 years. Successful mentoring pairs embrace the unique characteristics their age difference brings and use them to their advantage.

THE SURVEY SAYS

We identified a wide range of age combinations among the mentors and mereas we surveyed. Here we will organize the age combinations into four categories.

Mentoring relationships are categorized according to age combinations in which:

 a. the mentor is younger than or similar in age to her merea.
 b. the mentor is 2-20 years older than her merea.
 c. the mentor is 21-40 years older than her merea.
 d. the mentor is 41 or more years older than her merea.

When we looked at the age combinations in 177 mentoring relationships from our surveys, we found that in a majority of relationships the mentor was 2-20 years older (about 60 percent). In 20 percent of the relationships the mentor was 21-40 years older than her merea, with the remaining 20 percent of relationships being similarly divided between those having a similar-aged mentor and those in which the mentor was 41 or more years older.

Using the preceding four categories above as a guide, circle the age combination described for each mentor/merea relationship described below. Then for each age combination describe the benefits mentioned in the comment.

1. "She's the grandmother I never had. When she told me how she churned butter, I felt connected with women of another era. She has enriched my life and given me a heritage I will pass on to my own children."

Age category: a. b. c. d. Benefits: _____

2. "We can hang out together and she understands me because she's at a similar place in life. Problems with our children, our husbands—even our joys, our fears—all of them are about the same."

Age category: a. b. c. d. Benefits: _____

3. "My mentor is ahead of me by three decades. Since she's raised four children to adulthood, I figure she knows what she is talking about."

Age category: a. b. c. d. Benefits: _____

4. "My mentor is not quite one generation older than me, so she's far enough ahead to teach me from her experience, but not so far ahead that she can't identify with what I'm going through."

Age category: a. b. c. d. Benefits: _____

How did you match the age combinations with the descriptive comments? This is how we answered them: 1.d, 2.a, 3.c, 4.b. Each mentor/merea age combination brings unique blessings. Before you jump into your mentoring relationship headfirst, ground yourself in an understanding of the unique dynamics of each combination.

YOUNGER OR SIMILAR-AGED MENTOR

A merea will find certain advantages in having a mentor near her own age. Educators have long recognized the mutual benefit of peer mentoring. In Christian mentoring, mereas value mentors who are their age because they have so much in common. They speak the same slang because they approach life from the same developmental vantage point.

However, peer mentoring has certain disadvantages. Since both mentor and merea share the same developmental stage of life, the mentor has no more life experience chronologically than her merea. In addition, a similar-aged pair is more likely to socialize as friends, making it more difficult for the merea to view the mentor as a guide, advisor, and teacher.

MENTORING PAIRS 2–20 YEARS APART

One advantage for mentors and mereas separated by 2-20 years is that they are likely to still have many historical memories in common. For example, even though Edna wasn't a teenager in the era of bell-bottoms as I was, she does recall their being popular among the students she taught. (She admits that she even tried on a few pair.) A mentor less than 20 years older than her merea may still have comparable energy levels to bring to the relationship and the activities they enjoy together.

On the downside, a mentor less than 20 years older than her merea may not have garnered enough life or spiritual experience to approach her merea with wisdom. The mentor may still be on the fast track in her career as well as juggling responsibilities for home and children. Adding on the responsibility of mentoring may feel overwhelming.

MENTORING PAIRS 21–40 YEARS APART

When one to two generations separate the mentor/merea, the older mentor has had life experiences which the merea has not lived through. Possibly the mentor has walked through significant life passages such as rearing her children to adulthood, has relinquished or attained many of her career goals, and may even be nearing or already be in retirement. As family and career demands decrease, the mentor may find more time and energy to invest in the mentoring relationship.

On the other hand, mentors 21-40 years older, who are providing care for elderly parents, or who themselves are experiencing physical illness, may not have the free time they had hoped for. As energy levels begin to wane, they may not feel they can relate to a merea who juggles a hectic family schedule and career demands—one whose life is organized according to her daytimer.

MENTORING PAIRS SEPARATED BY 41 OR MORE YEARS

Mentors two or more generations older than their mereas offer rich history and heritage to their mereas. If in reasonably good health, the mentor can enjoy the vitality that the younger merea brings to the relationship. The merea's whole family, in fact, may adopt the mentor as a grandmother figure. If the merea encourages her mentor to review life events verbally, she will not only enrich her own understanding and wisdom, but she will also enable her mentor to give meaning and value to her life experiences.

Clearly, the merea's willingness to slow her pace to the mentor's will largely determine whether the relationship will flourish or wilt. The longer the relationship and the closer the pair becomes, the more likely the merea will grieve the loss of her mentor due to debilitating illness or death. Openly discussing this possibility (if both are comfortable doing so), will strengthen the bond between the two.

HOW RUTH AND NAOMI USED AGE DIFFERENCE TO THEIR ADVANTAGE

When it comes to female mentor/merea pairs making their age difference work for them, the Old Testament features Ruth and Naomi as its leading ladies. While we don't know their exact ages, we do know that Naomi viewed herself as too old to bear children (Ruth 1:11–12). We also know that Ruth had been married to Naomi's son (Ruth 1:4), and that Boaz was surprised that Ruth had not pursued younger men, probably those nearer her own age (Ruth 3:10). So the two may have been separated by at least a generation.

If so, in which of our age-combination categories would this pair fit?

Ruth and Naomi may have been from 21-40 years apart. Scriptures record how they each embraced the age characteristics the other brought to the relationship.

Read Ruth 3:1–5 and record evidence that Ruth trusted Naomi's years of experience.

Ruth listened to Naomi, deferred to her experience because she trusted her, and followed her instructions implicitly.

Ruth 2:17–19 describes Ruth's experience gathering grain in the field of Boaz. Read the passage and record evidence that Naomi benefited from Ruth's youthful energy.

_____

THE BLESSINGS OF YOUTH/THE BLESSINGS OF AGE

Read each of the following verses and unscramble the word next to it which describes an age-related quality that blessed Ruth and Naomi's relationship.

Ruth: Qualities of Youth that Blessed the Relationship

- Ruth 1:18—e a t e t d n i i m n r o   _____

- Ruth 2:2—t s s d u n i i o r u   _____

- Ruth 2:11—a a n i t m s   _____

Naomi: Qualities of Age That Blessed the Relationship

- Ruth 2:22—m w d o i s   _____

- Ruth 3:2–4—w e d l e g o n k   _____

- Ruth 3:18—e e t c a p n i   _____

How did you do? Look at Ruth's youthful characteristics first. Ruth's refusal to leave Naomi hints at her *determination*. Youth often brings a zeal that energizes a friendship. I can't help but think that Naomi leaned hard on Ruth's determined spirit to get her through her own time of grief and bitterness at the loss of her husband and sons (Ruth 2:20–21). When Ruth offered to gather grain, she showed how *industrious* she was. While this trait probably revealed her integrity as a person as much as an age characteristic, it does reflect a youthful let's-do-it attitude. Ruth worked in the fields from morning until night gathering grain. Talk about *stamina*! Since Naomi's strength was waning, and she had no one to provide for her, Ruth's ability to stay with the task until she had an ample amount of grain for both of them may have saved Naomi's life.

Naomi sported a spry and savvy attitude. What she didn't possess in physical prowess she made up for in insight and ingenuity. She showed *wisdom* and an understanding of the ways of the world when she advised Ruth to glean only in the safety of Boaz's field. Her advice to Ruth on how to approach Boaz as a potential marriage candidate demonstrated her thorough *knowledge* of Jewish law. Aging brings a slower pace and often with it, *patience*. What a gift Naomi gave Ruth when she taught her how to wait.

Your awareness of the effects of your and your merea's age difference will enhance the quality of your relationship. The principles we have shared are just that: principles, not rules. Integrate those which directly apply to you, and do not be alarmed if a characteristic of your relationship defines the exception to the rule.

For instance, while Edna is 17 years my senior, her high energy level makes me tired. However, embracing our age difference means I caution her as she walks over slippery ground. She picks up dishes I have left lying about, and I help her find lost items since my short-term memory is much more acute. Now . . . where is my pen?

———— Always Remember, Never Forget ————

While youth demands "doing," age whispers "being." Success in your relationship is determined by how you balance the two.

CHAPTER EIGHTEEN
From Covenant to Closure

Mentoring is like being a potter's helper, watching God, the Potter, fashion a beautiful vessel for service.

The Potter's Wheel

Lord, Jane is on the Potter's wheel,
I have climbed right up there with her.
Watched you molding her with skill,
Guarding her from Satan's slither.

I was there when her son died,
Held her when she feared the night,
Quietly I stood beside,
Interceding in her fight.

She's a stronger woman now,
Infused with joy and self-esteem,
A vessel, fit, which You endowed
With gifts, fulfilling Your own dream.

Lord, the time has gone so fast;
I've been whirling, spinning, reeling.
Now we're slowing down at last,
But closure excavates mixed feelings.

Look! My hair is standing on its end,
Empty pockets, books I've lent her...
Yet...Lord, I long to start again;
For Your glory let me mentor!

—© 1998 Edna Ellison

Read Jeremiah 18:1–6 and write what God tells you about His working in your mentoring relationship.

_____

_____

_____

Like Jeremiah, you will listen to God, go to the Potter's house, and watch Him mold His handiwork until it is fit to serve Him.

God will guide you in the mentoring process. He is in control. Listen to Him. Watch Him work in a life needing molding and shaping. Like your merea, you, too, are on the Potter's wheel.

LEAVING A LEGACY

Closure is a word often used to describe an ending point or completion in a relationship. Can you think of examples of closure in relationships described in the Bible? Moses and Joshua, David and Jonathan, and Paul and Timothy all experienced saying good-bye to each other.

Another example of closure occurs in 2 Kings 2:1–3, 5–6 when Elijah, the mentor, had to leave Elisha, his merea. **Read the passage looking for evidence that closure was difficult for Elijah and Elisha. Record your findings here.**

_____

_____

Saying good-bye is rarely easy. Elisha and Elijah's situation was no exception. Elisha showed the characteristic symptoms of separation anxiety, often experienced by a young child when Mother leaves. He clung to Elijah, refusing to leave his side. Elisha refused to speak of Elijah's imminent departure and wouldn't permit others to speak of it.

But as any good mother bird knows, the only way for Baby to fly is to kick him out of the nest. And fly he did. When God took Elijah up in a whirlwind to heaven, Elisha cried and tore his clothes in grief. Then he stooped to retrieve Elijah's fallen cloak. From the moment he picked up the cloak, Elisha soared. Even a group of prophets nearby acknowledged Elisha's blessing: "The spirit of Elijah is resting on Elisha" (2 Kings 2:15).

GREATER THINGS YOU WILL DO

Following in his mentor's path and vision, Elisha performed miraculous deeds after Elijah was taken up.

List miracles he performed as recorded in the following verses.

2 Kings 2:19–20 _____

2 Kings 4:4–6 _____

2 Kings 4:32–37 _____

2 Kings 4:41 _____

2 Kings 4:42–44 _____

2 Kings 5:1–14 _____

2 Kings 6:5–6 _____

2 Kings 7:1–2,17–18 _____

What a repertoire of miracles! Elisha purified polluted water, enhanced the oil supply, raised a boy from the dead, purified contaminated food, fed 100 people, healed a leper, caused iron to float, and prophesied. Elisha even performed a miracle after his own death. Read 2 Kings 13:21 for the post-death miracle. (Caution: Don't expect this of yourself or your merea!)

THE LAW OF DIMINISHING EXPERTISE

The moment you enter the mentoring relationship your goal will be to mentor your merea into maturity. Just as a mother aims to see her child eventually independent of her, you will strengthen your merea through your nurturing, guiding, and teaching, looking forward to the day she soars on her own. Christian speaker, Jill Brisco, calls this principle The Law of Diminishing Expertise; that is, as your merea grows in her expertise, you diminish yours accordingly.

Although, strictly speaking, John was not Jesus' mentor, he did pave the way for Jesus' ministry. Read John 3:30. How did John demonstrate The Law of Diminishing Expertise?

_____

_____

FROM CLOSURE TO COVENANT

Does the subheading From Closure to Covenant seem backward to you? Actually it illustrates the truth that although the mentoring relationship, as you know it, will end at some point, closure does not always mean leaving. Many times the relationship continues, but on a different level.

The pair renegotiates the terms of the relationship and reaches a new agreement (covenant). Sometimes the mentor and merea move into a peer relationship, sharing mutual interests. Perhaps each of you will mentor a new merea. (The former merea may seek advice from her mentor as the relationship continues in an entirely new form.) Occasionally, God blesses a merea so that she becomes a mentor to her former mentor, teaching her a special gift or truth.

Tricia and I have noticed this renegotiation process occurring naturally as our relationship has evolved. Read what Tricia recently wrote to me:

"For several years, Edna, you have taught me the finer points of writing, everything from what not to say to an editor, to how to use 'who' and 'whom' (I'm still working on this one. I'm to the point of saying, 'Whom cares anyway?'). However, when we were writing together not long ago, I noticed how much I edited your work. At one point, I scribbled so many red lines on one of your chapters that you dumped it and started over. (I think the power went to my head.)

"I'm not implying that I have arrived at some all-knowing juncture. You still have to show me how to use the rat (or was that a mouse?) on the computer. But we both are growing. We are proof that, 'As iron sharpens iron, so one man sharpens another' (Prov. 27:17). In fact, we sharpen each other so much that I now find myself reluctant to write without you in the room as my sounding board. We have become colleagues. I know you rejoice as I do at how the Lord works during our writing times together."

Jesus, too, faced closure and renegotiation of relationships when He left His earthly ministry.

Scan John 14:16–28 and describe the ways that the relationship between Jesus and His followers would change and ultimately grow.

_____

_____

Jesus said that soon He would not only walk with them as on earth, but He would actually live within them. In order for the new phase of the relationship to begin, closure would need to be completed and the old ways of relating would end.

RITES OF PASSAGE

Whatever the terms of the renegotiated relationship, closure represents a significant passage. Recognition in some form establishes a rite of passage and provides a sense of completion.

Jesus prepared His followers for closure with two promises. Read John 14:17–19 and write the promises which comforted the disciples and acknowledged their time of passage.

Whether you choose a public or private recognition, individually or jointly with other mentor/merea pairs, honor your merea in a fitting way.

Check the following rites of passage you may use during the closure phase of your mentor/merea relationship.

- ❑ I plan to give a challenge, as Paul did in Ephesians 4:20–21.
- ❑ I will honor her by some form of public recognition at church.
- ❑ I will give a parting gift to remind her of our special time together.
- ❑ I will have given her spiritual gifts; that is more important than a physical gift.
- ❑ I will send a thank-you note to her, for being my merea.
- ❑ I will remember her birthday and other special occasions.
- ❑ I will be relieved when the responsibility ends.
- ❑ I plan to write a poem, a song, or another writing keepsake to her.
- ❑ I will keep a scrapbook of our time together to present to her.

Habakkuk 1:5 says, "Look at the nations and watch and be utterly amazed. For I am going to do something in your days that you would not believe, even if you were told." Praise God for what He is about to do in your merea's life. Then sit back and watch her fly!

—————— **Always Remember, Never Forget** ——————

We don't recommend kicking her out of the nest,
but a little push might not be a bad idea!

Mentoring requires a depth of giving, honesty, and vulnerability that few other relationships in life demand. The up-close-and-personal, and sometimes intense, nature of the ministry places mentors at high risk for frustration and burnout. Regular support group meetings with other mentors provide a safe haven where nurturing and encouragement allow mentors to process the challenges and joys of the mentoring experience.

The mentor, like her merea, is on a journey toward wholeness and completion in Christ. Studying with other mentors holds each mentor accountable for pursuing internally her own healing and passionate relationship with the Savior. Furthermore, the support group serves as a constant reminder that all mentoring of eternal value grows from honesty and one's fullness in Christ.

GETTING STARTED

If this book is distributed at the first meeting, follow the guidelines for the introductory session. Remind each group member to bring a Bible, a pencil, and her personal copy of *Woman to Woman: Preparing Yourself to Mentor* to each session.

The suggested questions may be used to guide discussion during regular meetings with mentors. Although the frequency of meetings can be determined by the group, most groups find that meeting regularly once a week is most effective.

You may use the following questions to stimulate thought and discussion within the group. Do not feel compelled to answer all of the questions. Rather customize the questions to fit the needs and interests of your group.

If your mentors' group meets weekly after individually studying one chapter a day, then you may choose one or two questions from each chapter to address during your session. If your mentors are completing one or two chapters per week, then you may have time to discuss all of the study questions for each chapter and discuss other issues raised during your individual study during the week.

Each session ends with a list of potential prayer issues. Group members may choose to pray about the most pressing issues facing them or write their own. During the prayer time members may wish to pray about their own needs silently. Another option is to have members pair off, sharing their needs and praying for each other.

HINTS FOR ENHANCING THE GROUP DISCUSSION EXPERIENCE

While group discussion sounds simple enough, the dynamics of a discussion can career out of control if someone specific is not directing the discussion. Choose someone to lead each session. If you do not have a mentor support team or facilitator who leads each week, take turns serving as the group facilitator. A facilitator is someone who leads by encouragement. She encourages group members to share their feelings, sets limits on more talkative members by asking for responses from quieter members, and is sensitive to time constraints by refocusing the discussion when the group loses direction.

Be prepared for a wide variety of responses to certain questions as emotions are evoked during the discussion of sensitive, painful, or even joyful issues. Two members may express opposite feelings about a similar experience. Demonstrate respect for the validity of each person's internal experience. Negative or intense emotions will often dissipate when acknowledged: "I can tell that you feel overwhelmed by that demand on you."

When someone expresses a fear or other concern, avoid minimizing or nullifying those comments. If a group member says, "I'm afraid I won't know the answer to my merea's Bible questions. I don't know that much about the Bible," avoid responding, "Oh, you know plenty. I've heard you talk in Sunday School." Also avoid platitudes such as, "Well, just trust in the Lord and He will guide you."

How can you respond in a helpful way that encourages each member to identify, acknowledge, and clarify her feelings, then examine those feelings and concerns in the light of the truth?

Just as in responding to the expression of opinion or emotion, acknowledge the validity of the concern. You may accomplish this by:

- looking at the person while she is talking.
- concentrating on what she is saying and what it means to her.
- nodding (to show understanding, not necessarily agreement).
- encouraging her to expand on her concern with, "Go on," or "Yes," or "I'd like to know a little more."
- gently asking for clarification when needed, "I'm not sure I understood what you mean."

In a support group, members entrust their inner selves—their thoughts, experiences, and feelings—to the care of group members. This is risky and most of us feel a little awkward about the experience at first. One way to build group trust is for members to agree that anything verbalized within the group will be kept private within the group. Mentors will soon face the challenge of maintaining privacy when interacting with their mereas. The mentor support group sessions provide an excellent practice field for dealing with issues of privacy.

Picture a nugget of self-disclosure as a precious jewel you've been asked to take care of when the owner leaves for a trip. Even if you are very cautious when you let someone else look at and hold it, the jewel may be smudged or chipped. When you return the damaged jewel to the owner she will feel grief and betrayal, even though that was not your intent. For further help on the subject, preview Chapter 14—Building Trust through Accountability and Confidentiality.

A Final Reminder: It is possible that during the course of this study some women will realize that they should not mentor at this time. Make sure that the group affirms each person's responsibility and right to make this decision for herself. Remind the group that changing one's mind about mentoring is not a failure; in fact, it may mean the Lord is calling a person into a different ministry or that, although the person will be a mentor, the timing is not right. Permission to discontinue the study or the mentoring ministry must be affirmed by the whole group so that guilt will not be a motivator for service, as women respond to pressure rather than the call of God.

GETTING TO KNOW YOU SURVEY

SUPPLIES

Bibles, pencils, Woman to Woman: Preparing Yourself to Mentor (for every session these are referred to as "minimum").

1. Ask each member to complete the following survey. Respond to the following questions (choose only one answer for each):

If I had a jar of marshmallow cream, I would:

    A. give it to the homeless.
    B. eat it all at one sitting.
    C. make fudge.
    D. use it for paste.

When it comes to plants and gardening, I'd be most likely to:

    A. leave the weeds and go get pizza.
    B. don my gardening garb at 5:30 A.M. to beat the heat.
    C. buy a new fern instead of trying revive a puny one.
    D. prune the roses while dressed in my nightshirt tucked in my shorts.

If a 65-pound dog were walking toward me, I'd say:

    A. "Get away from me, you slobbering carnivorous canine."
    B. "I'm outta' here."
    C. "I'll pet you as long as you don't put your head on my lap."
    D. "Come here pooch and I'll share my marshmallow cream."

If someone asked me to define "periscope man," I'd say he was:

    A. a sailor who works on a submarine looking outside through that long tube thing.
    B. a proctologist.
    C. a guy with a long neck.
    D. a man who holds his water glass at eye level, squints, and sights the other side of the glass across the water's surface.

What I'd like to know about mentoring:

    A. Nothing. If I put one more thing in my head, I think it'll explode.

B. Everything. How to get one; how to be one; how to start a mentoring ministry; you name it, I want to know it. Call me a human sponge for information.

C. Where was one when I needed her?

D. The bottom line: What will I have to do?

Discuss your answers and get to know one another.

1. Read aloud:
   Mentoring is an exciting, fun adventure. In *Woman to Woman: Preparing Yourself to Mentor*, marshmallow cream, gardening attire, a 65-pound dog, and the periscope man make their appearances in the personal experiences Tricia and Edna share. So while you're learning, take the opportunity to laugh with each other—a lot. It will get you through some pretty tough times, even when the eggs blow up (Chapter 6)!

2. Review together the "Introduction" of *Woman to Woman: Preparing Yourself to Mentor*.

3. Review the "Table of Contents." Allow a few minutes for members to scan the chapter titles and content.

4. Which chapter titles make you respond with "Yes! That's What I Need!"?

5. Which chapters look the most intimidating to you?

6. Decide how many chapters mentors are to study before each group session.

7. Discuss as a group how you will use time during the group sessions. Sessions may include group discussion, prayer time, fellowship, and refreshments.

8. Determine your meeting schedule.

9. Remind members to bring Bibles, Woman to Woman: Preparing Yourself to Mentor, and pencils to each session.

PRAYER NEEDS:

- I need the Lord to help me concentrate on the studies so that I can absorb what He's trying to teach me.
- I need self-discipline to complete what I have started.
- I want to thank the Lord for this opportunity to serve and grow.

UNIT ONE
Preparing Your Heart

CHAPTER ONE
Do I Have the Stuff Mentors Are Made Of?

SUPPLIES

3-by-5-inch cards, pencils, dry-erase board or chalkboard, marker or chalk, basket, refreshments (optional for each session)

1. The list of mentoring definitions includes quotes from women who completed our surveys as well as some respected authors on mentoring. Which definition of mentoring did you choose? Why that particular one?

ME, A MENTOR?

2. Share with the group your own definition of mentoring. As you listen to other definitions, add any ideas to your definition in the margin of your book.

3. What feelings have you experienced about mentoring someone? In what ways are your feelings similar to those of other mentors in the group?

4. Discuss the concerns group members express about mentoring.
   List the concerns on a dry-erase board or chalkboard. How can group members encourage one another and respond to one another's concerns? Write down in the margin of your book the fears and concerns mentioned by other women in the group. Pray that the Lord will meet those needs specifically. You may stop and pray for one another at this time.

COMPETING WITH THE TITUS 2 WOMAN

5. Read Titus 2:3 together. How did you feel after reading the requirements of Titus 2:3?

QUALIFIED AND CALLED

6. How did your expectations of yourself change as you checked the characteristics list under "Qualified and Called"?

FROM RESISTANCE TO RESOLVE

7. Read aloud Exodus 3:7–10 and 4:10–12, with group members taking turns sharing their responses to the "But Lord…_____." Ask each group member to write her "But Lord…" responses on a piece of paper or

card with her name on it. Place all the cards in a basket or bag and let each group member take one (not her own). Ask each member to tuck the card into the next week's study portion of her book as a reminder to pray for those specific concerns.

PRAYER NEEDS:
- I need courage to acknowledge and receive support to walk through my fears and concerns about mentoring.
- I need direction from the Holy Spirit about my call to mentor.
- I need strength to look at myself honestly as the study progresses.
- I want to risk being transparent and share my true self with the group and with God.

CHAPTER TWO
Me, Gifted?

SUPPLIES
Minimum plus paper, 3-by-5-inch cards, pencils, basket

1. Read Ephesians 4:11–16. Share God's purpose in gifting each of His children.

UNIQUELY GIFTED
2. When someone says, "You are gifted!" what is your first thought response? Write your thought response to that comment on a card (no name). Place your card with other members' cards in a basket and mix them. Each person should take one and read it aloud. How are responses similar? Different?
3. Take turns sharing one natural gift and how it may be used in mentoring.
4. Take turns sharing one learned gift and how it may be used in mentoring.
5. Review the list of spiritual gifts. Take turns sharing one spiritual gift and how it may be used in mentoring. (If you have not identified your spiritual gift(s), get input from other members of the group as to what they see in you.)
6. Write your name at the top of a piece of paper (all members do this).

Pass each person's paper around for group members to write what they see and appreciate in that person. Descriptions may include natural, learned, or spiritual gifts as well as specific attitudes and actions. Return each member's completed paper to her.

UNIQUELY YOU

7. Why do we compare ourselves, including our gifts, attributes and physical selves, with others?
8. How does comparing yourself to someone else affect the joy you experience in what the Lord has given and is doing uniquely in you?

PRAYER NEEDS:

- It's hard for me to see myself as gifted.
- I want the Lord to reveal my giftedness to me.
- I want to acknowledge and embrace my giftedness.
- I want my giftedness to meet the unique needs of my merea.

CHAPTER THREE
What's in It for Me?

SUPPLIES
Minimum

1. Review together the illustration about Megan and Anne at the beginning of this chapter.

TAKING A HARD LOOK AT MOTIVES

2. How did you feel after reading Anne's experience?
3. Why is it important to discern your motives before you begin mentoring?
4. Share sources of pressure that may cause group members to feel a need to perform.
5. Review together the section, "Avoiding the Pitfalls." Identify and discuss the pitfalls most likely to be a problem for you.

PRAYING ABOUT YOUR MOTIVES

6. Read aloud together Psalm 139:23–24 (KJV):

"Search me, O God, and know my heart: try me, and know my thoughts: And see if there be any wicked way in me, and lead me in the way everlasting."

PRAYER NEEDS:

- I want the Lord to reveal ulterior motives that soil my purest motives for mentoring.
- I need to be freed from the pressure of trying to earn others' approval or admiration.
- I need forgiveness and courage to face those pitfalls most likely to be a problem for me.

CHAPTER FOUR
Where Do I Grow from Here?

SUPPLIES
Minimum

SELF-EVALUATION OR SPIRIT ILLUMINATION
1. In what ways have you experienced feelings similar to Tricia's feelings about self-evaluation?
2. How does self-evaluation differ from Holy Spirit illumination in terms of: purpose? method? outcome?

ALL GROWN UP AND NO PLACE TO GO?
3. Discuss the results of the "Ready or Not Survey." Did you experience doubts about your readiness to mentor as a result of completing the survey? If so, you may share your concerns with the group and request prayer that the Lord will reveal His will for you. Be supportive to others who may question whether they should mentor at this time. Don't minimize concerns. Affirm the Holy Spirit's willingness and ability to reveal His plan and timing for each woman's mentoring ministry.

GETTING TO THE HEART OF THE MATTER
4. When you visualize the scene in Isaiah 40:11, how do you feel? Share how

the scene affects you when you picture yourself as the lamb and Christ the shepherd.

5. As you completed the "Heart Search Questionnaire," which question touched you the most? Why?

6. Are you brokenhearted about any habit, attitude, or spiritual immaturity in your life? Share with the group, if you feel comfortable.

PRAYER NEEDS:

- I need release from self-evaluation that leads to my dwelling on failures and makes me feel disgust with myself.
- I need to believe I am fully acceptable to God just as I am.
- I confess that I have a problem bigger than my ability to control it. I want the Holy Spirit to shine His light on the dark crevices of my heart and allow His grace to free me.

CHAPTER FIVE
What Exactly Does a Mentor Do?

SUPPLIES

Minimum plus dry-erase board or chalkboard (optional for #1, #2, & #3), chalk or marker

MENTORING ROLES

1. Name the five mentoring roles without looking at your book. Divide into two teams and take turns stating a descriptive behavior and asking the other team to identify the role to which the behavior belongs.

2. In which role would you feel the most comfortable? How could you use your giftedness in that role to support another mentor who feels apprehensive about the role?

3. List the names and roles in which other group members say they are most comfortable. (Make notes in the margin of your own book for future reference.)

4. Identify the role that makes you most apprehensive. How could another mentor friend help you strengthen that area? You may refer to the list you made in #3.

RECEIVING WHAT YOU GIVE

5. In what ways have you received the ministries of service, encouragement, teaching, wise counsel, and guidance from others? How have these prepared you to serve as a mentor?

REACHING IN BEFORE REACHING OUT

6. As you consider the challenge to "receive ministry to your own needs while you learn to mentor another," share one area of your life in which you need to be served, taught, encouraged, counseled, or guided.

PRAYER NEEDS:

*   I need discernment as to which areas I need help and support in order to mentor.
*   I am uncomfortable with the role: _____. I want to find ways to strengthen myself in that area.
*   Looking at this chapter makes mentoring seem like an overwhelming task. I need peace to release responsibility for "doing it all" to the Lord.

UNIT TWO
The Scope of Your Ministry

CHAPTER SIX
Mentoring as a Servant

SUPPLIES
Minimum plus coin, tabletop, local telephone books, paper, pencils

TWO SIDES OF THE SAME COIN

1. Spin a coin on the tabletop (or flip a coin). Heads=Leading; Tails=Serving. Take turns sharing one word which describes either a leader or a servant, whichever side comes up (refer to the list of characteristics).
2. What do you think servant leader means?

SERVING ON YOUR KNEES

3. Read John 13:2 and describe the scene Jesus faced. How would you have responded in the upstairs room scene with the disciples?
4. Read John 13:1,3. Explain what this phrase means: *Jesus knew*. If you knew what Jesus knew, how would that affect your mentoring?

SERVING AS A MAJOR DOMO

5. How is a mentor like a major domo?
6. Use the telephone book and personal contacts of group members to list resources you may use to meet the following needs:

❑ Clothes   ❑ Shelter for battered women   ❑ Mental Health Services

❑ Food   ❑ Abused children   ❑ Chemical Dependency

❑ Job resources   ❑ Family Social Services   ❑ Other (brainstorm other ideas)

❑ Medical Care   ❑ Counseling   _____

7. Assign each group member the task of identifying community resources to meet each of the needs listed above. This may be done within or outside of group time. When feasible, call and request information from specific identified local services. Bring to the next session and share with the group. Compile a community resource file for mentors. Add to the file as needed.

PRAYER NEEDS:

*   I want the Lord to give me a servant's heart and attitude.
*   I need to open my eyes to my merea's needs.
*   I'm committed to learning the resources available in the community.

CHAPTER SEVEN
Mentoring as an Encourager

SUPPLIES
Minimum

1. Has God ever asked you to do something you did not want to do as He did Edna before she spoke at the YMCA? What did you do?
2. Share ways persons have encouraged you in your life.

THE ENCOURAGER WITHIN

3. Which tools of encouragement from the "High-Five List" are you most likely to use to minister to your merea?
4. Can you think of other ways you might encourage your merea?

THE VISION OF VICTORY

5. Based on Judges 4 and 5, describe what you think Deborah's personality was like.
6. Describe ways Deborah encouraged Barak.

THE REALITY OF VICTORY

7. Describe specific examples in which encouraging words and actions could be used by God to give victory in your merea's life.

PRAYER NEEDS:

- I need to find the encourager within.
- I want to focus more on the positive baby steps that my merea takes rather than her failures or immaturity.
- I need encouragement right now to face a trial in my own life. The most encouraging words I could hear right now would be:

CHAPTER EIGHT
Mentoring as a Teacher

SUPPLIES

Minimum plus dry-erase board or chalkboard, marker or chalk, eraser

1. Review the introduction as a group. How do think the new Christian, Becky, felt when she did not understand church rules and no one could show her exactly where they were?

WHAT DO I TEACH?

2. How would you answer the question, "What do I teach?" Discuss and list on the board Bible studies and other resource materials that might be useful for mentoring.
3. Share with the group a favorite verse which may be helpful to your merea as she strives toward spiritual maturity.

4. Identify unspoken rules in your church, part of your church culture, which a new Christian might find confusing. Have you ever questioned some of the rules?

5. Share one life principle you have learned from experience that would be helpful to teach your merea.

WHERE DO I TEACH?

6. Share places that might be suitable for studying the Bible together with your merea.

WHEN DO I TEACH?

7. Review together Tricia's illustration about how her mom used a "teachable moment" with Emily, Tricia's daughter. Describe a teachable moment in your life. How does focusing on the teachable moment affect the way you will teach your merea?

HOW DO I TEACH?

8. Review as a group "The Loving Teacher" questionnaire. Which one of the characteristics of a loving teacher is the most difficult for you?

PRAYER NEEDS:

- I need confidence in my ability to teach.
- I don't feel I know enough of the Bible to teach.
- I need to set aside time for my own Bible study before I can teach someone else.
- I need wisdom to discern what, where, when, and how to teach.

CHAPTER NINE
Mentoring as a Counselor

SUPPLIES
Minimum plus dry-erase board or chalkboard, marker or chalk, eraser

1. Chapter 9 begins by mentioning "our deepest battles." Discuss battles that you or others you know have faced.

THE NEED AND THE CALL

2. On what grounds can nonprofessionals counsel others?

3. Read Galatians 6:2. What did you list as examples of burdens a merea may share?

A COUNSELOR IS SOMEONE WHO...

4. Write on the board characteristics which you and other group members identified desirable for a counselor. "I would look for someone who..."

WHAT COUNSELING IS AND IS NOT

5. Read the illustration about Tricia and her friend who was hurt by unkind words. What does it mean to "surf on someone else's wave of emotion"? Why is it dangerous?

DEFINING THE ROLE OF COUNSELOR

6. Using the definition in the "Defining the Role of Counselor" section as a guide, work as a group to write your own definition of counselor. Write it on the board.

THE LOST ART OF LISTENING

7. What reasons did you give for not listening? Listen to others' answers. Discuss suggestions for dealing with these distractions.

PREPARING YOURSELF AS A COUNSELOR

8. Read James 1:5 together. Pair off. Write down your greatest challenge in becoming the counselor you want to be. Share with your partner your neediness. Pray for each other's needs.

PRAYER NEEDS:

- I need confidence that I have something to offer another person in counseling.
- I want to listen better.
- I need to be able to stand back and not get caught up in another's emotion so much that I can't help her.
- I long for wisdom, not to have the right answer, but to respond the way God wants.

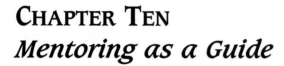

CHAPTER TEN
Mentoring as a Guide

SUPPLIES
Minimum plus dry-erase board or chalkboard, marker or chalk, eraser

1. Review the introduction. Read as a group Numbers 32:11–12. Discuss changes you each will need to make in order to serve God wholeheartedly.

GUIDE HER TO SPIRITUAL CLOSENESS WITH GOD
2. What is significant about Joshua accompanying Moses near the mountaintop to receive the Ten Commandments?

GUIDE HER BY MODELING THE ROLE
3. Without giving details, share with other mentors the truths you learned from a painful failure. How would these truths be helpful to a merea?

GUIDE HER WHERE YOU'VE BEEN
4. Joshua and the other guides traveled up into hill country to get a better perspective on the land they wanted to conquer. In your own life, how do you "get on a higher plane" for a better perspective on life?
5. Joshua studied the background of the people in the land. Brainstorm ways you may get to know your merea's background. How will this understanding affect how you mentor her?
6. Pair with someone, and recite Psalm 139:9–10 to each other from memory. Share an experience in your life when it seemed like you were "on the far side of the sea." How did God's hand guide you even there?
7. What does the ARNF mean: "You can guide someone only where you've been"?

PRAYER NEEDS:
- I want the Lord to give me a new perspective on _____
- I need courage to allow myself to be transparent enough to fail in front of others.
- I need the Lord's help in memorizing helpful Scriptures such as Psalm 139:9–10.
- I want to deepen my knowledge of Christ and His ways.

UNIT THREE
Keys to Building a Dynamic Duo

CHAPTER ELEVEN
Taking Off the Mask

SUPPLIES

Minimum plus copy of *The Velveteen Rabbit* (optional)

1. Read aloud the whole section from *The Velveteen Rabbit* alluded to in the first paragraph of this chapter. What does it mean to you to be "REAL"?
2. The introduction explains how strong a motivator self-preservation can be. Have you ever surprised yourself when you suddenly realized how strong your sense of self-preservation is? Can you share an experience that illustrates this point?
3. Share your responses to the questions about masked and real behaviors.

HELP! MY HALO IS FALLING

4. In what areas of your life are you tempted to keep your mask on and your halo perfectly balanced?

TAKING OFF THE MASK IS HARD

5. Describe Naaman. Do you know any "Naamans"? How are you like Naaman?
6. Tell about a time you were humiliated like Naaman (your halo was falling), but the experience made you more down-to-earth.

PRAYER NEEDS:

- I want to better understand what it means to be real in my life.
- I want to release the areas of my life about which I feel most insecure to the care of the Lord.
- I confess my need to be liked or admired in order to feel good about me. I want to feel special because of who I am in Christ, not because of what I have, what I look like, or how well I behave.

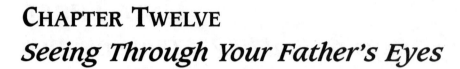

CHAPTER TWELVE
Seeing Through Your Father's Eyes

SUPPLIES
Minimum

PEOPLE LIKE ME
1. Describe someone who would be opposite of you.
2. Which lifestyle characteristics would make you feel most awkward with your merea?

A NEW WAY OF LOOKING AT PEOPLE
3. Using the descriptions from questions #1 and #2, share with the group how Jesus may view the characteristics you find most unlovely or intimidating.
4. How does seeing those characteristics as Christ might see them affect how you will respond to that person?

MINISTERING TO THE UP AND OUT
5. Describe a person whom you would view as "out of your league."

UP CLOSE AND PERSONAL
6. Read Edna's story about her husband, the "periscope man." Do you see annoying traits in someone you love? How have you learned to deal with these challenging traits?

SEEING EYE-TO-EYE
7. Review together Tricia's experience about how easily a condescending attitude can damage a relationship. Share your responses to the questions about how viewing your merea through your Father's eyes will change the way you respond in specific situations. Read each accompanying Scripture passage aloud.

PRAYER NEEDS:
- I need a cleansed view of how God sees me. I want to replace my faulty and negative perception with God's truth about how special, lovely, and worthy I am, and I want to share this new view of self with my merea.
- I want to be able to accept others' eccentricities and failures without judging them harshly.
- I want to give understanding to my merea when she responds in ways that disappoint or frustrate me.

CHAPTER THIRTEEN
Developing Heart-Core Intimacy

SUPPLIES
Minimum

1. Read aloud from the introduction Edna's story of the loss of her husband and its effect on her relationship with her daughter, Patsy. What does "heart-core intimacy" look like to you; that is, how would you recognize it if you saw it?

THE BOND OF COMMON GROUND
2. Read aloud the experience of Walker (see "Life Traditions"). Describe a life tradition which bonds you with another person.
3. Read aloud Tricia's experience being a preacher's kid (see "Life Experiences"). Describe a life experience which bonds you with another person.
4. Read silently as a group Luke 1:11–38. Discuss ways in which Mary's and Elizabeth's experiences showed that they "shared the language and feeling of God's heart" (see Esther Burroughs's comment under "Spiritual Experiences"). Describe a spiritual experience which bonds you with another person.

THE BOND OF SHARED EVENTS
5. Share an experience with someone that made a special memory for you.
6. Read Tricia's story of a "Shared Humor" experience with her mom. Can you recall a humorous experience which triggers laughter between you and another person?
7. Review Tricia and Edna's example of how they celebrate each one's unique approach to life (see "Celebrating Uniqueness"). Describe one relationship in which you celebrate uniqueness. How have you turned frustration with idiosyncrasies into something you can celebrate?
8. What can you do to find common ground, build a storehouse of shared memories, and celebrate the differences between you and your merea?

PRAYER NEEDS:
* I need understanding of my merea's life experiences, even if those experiences have not been my own.
* I want to be able to discern my merea's spiritual needs and find spiritual common ground on which to build.
* I will need patience to be able to celebrate uniqueness instead of becoming frustrated by our differences.

CHAPTER FOURTEEN
Building Trust Through Accountability and Confidentiality

SUPPLIES
Minimum plus dry-erase board or chalkboard, marker or chalk, eraser. Consider inviting a pastoral staff member as a resource for part of this session.

ACCOUNTABILITY
1. List on the board issues group members identified for which mentors and mereas are answerable to one another. In the margin add other mentors' suggestions to your own list.

CONFIDENTIALITY
2. Share which option you chose as your guiding principle for maintaining privacy. With other group members, write on the board ideas for handling privacy issues. Document a group philosophy for how mentors will deal with issues of privacy. Consult your pastoral staff if you need additional guidance.

DEALING WITH ISSUES OF PRIVACY
3. What is the twofold purpose of keeping information shared between mentor and merea private?
4. Read aloud the first four paragraphs of this section (p. 80). Why do mentors need the assurance of privacy just as mereas? Discuss when and how each mentor will talk with her merea about the expectation and promise of privacy. Review the mentor/merea covenant on page 132 and personalize it according to your needs.

THIS MATTER OF TRUST
5. If you had a mentor, what character traits would help you to trust her with your true self?
6. Read aloud Proverbs 25:19. What does this verse say to you about how you relate to your merea?

COVENANT FRIENDSHIP
7. How is the mentor/merea relationship similar to David and Jonathan's relationship?

THE RELATIONSHIP BETWEEN TRUST AND YOUR MEREA'S SPIRITUAL GROWTH
8. Review together "Leaning to Learning: Steps of a Merea's Growth." How can you as a mentor help your merea grow?

PRAYER NEEDS:
- I find it hard to keep promises (like being on time for meetings). I want to be someone my merea can count on.
- I desire to provide the safe haven for my merea that I would expect in a friend.
- I need wisdom and discipline to keep information shared in the mentoring relationship private.

UNIT FOUR
Keeping Your Balance

CHAPTER FIFTEEN
The How and Why of Boundaries

SUPPLIES
Minimum plus dry-erase board or chalkboard, markers or chalk, eraser

1. Have you ever felt pressured to respond to a need when you did not feel ready or able to do so? Read aloud the illustration about Tonie in the introduction. Share how you would have responded to that specific situation.

ABOUT FENCES AND NEIGHBORS
2. Read Tricia's story about how she learned the value of having your own space. Do you believe that "good fences make good neighbors"? Share with the group why or why not.

WHAT IS A BOUNDARY?
3. Have you ever felt awkward when someone talked too closely in your face? Tell how you felt.
4. At what point in your life did you recognize your beliefs as your own?
5. Refer to the section "Spiritual Boundaries." Read Revelation 3:20 together. How does God show respect for your spiritual boundaries?

LIMIT-SETTING AS A LOVING ACTION

6. God shows His love by setting limits on us. In what ways is limit-setting a loving action toward your merea? Toward yourself?

LIES THAT TAKE YOU IN AND BURN YOU OUT

7. Which one of the "Lies That Take You In" did you most identify with?

RESPONDING TO THE DEMANDS OF OTHERS:

8. Read the illustration in which Leslie, the merea, expects Kim, her mentor, to be always available (see "I'm Not a Good Mentor Unless..."). As a group, brainstorm and write on the board guilt-provoking or demanding statements a merea might say to her mentor.

9. Pair off and practice. One partner makes a demanding or guilt-provoking statement similar to those listed by the group, and the other partner practices responding firmly but lovingly according to the guidelines recommended in this section.

PRAYER NEEDS:

- I realize that my boundaries are weak. I always thought that looking out for myself was selfish.I need the Lord to clarify this truth for me.

- It's hard for me to picture boundary-setting as a loving action. I need help in order to set boundaries without experiencing overwhelming guilt.

- I need strength to overcome the temptation to believe the following lie (describe your own or choose one from "Lies That Take You In and Burn You Out").

- I want to grow in my ability to discern when and how to set boundaries/limits.

CHAPTER SIXTEEN
Keeping Your Well Full

SUPPLIES
Minimum

NO TIME FOR REFILLS

1. Read Edna's introduction aloud. Can you recall times when you were overextended in your service?

FILL IT UP, PLEASE

2   Read Proverbs 4:23 as a group. Why is it so important that you "watch over your heart"?

3. How do you think your own spiritual condition will affect how you mentor your merea?

LIVING WATER

4. Using the matching exercise, identify ways in which the characteristics of physical water mirror those of spiritual water.

FLOWING WATER

5. Read aloud John 4:11 and John 4:14. What is the difference between a *phrear* and a *pege*?

OPENING THE FLOW

6. Which "well-filling" activities did you identify as ones you often participate in? Can you think of others not listed?

7. What is a prayer triplet and how can it help you as a mentor?

8. Share the areas in your life for which you most need prayer. In the margin, make notes of prayer needs mentioned by other group members. Write in a place that will remind you to pray in the coming week.

A MATTER OF IMPORTANCE

9. Ask one group member to read aloud the poem "Keep My Well Full of Water."

PRAYER NEEDS:

*   In terms of service, I feel as if I'm doing everything but not doing anything well. I need to reevaluate my commitments.

*   I tend to first think of what I need to do to be a good mentor before I consider my own spiritual needs. I need to focus more on my own relationship with Christ and let my mentoring flow from that fullness.

*   I'm wondering if mentoring would cause me to be overextended. I need to discern the Lord's will regarding this area of service.

CHAPTER SEVENTEEN
Age Difference Makes a Difference

SUPPLIES
Minimum

1. Read the introduction together. In what ways do you believe life experience is more valuable than textbook knowledge?

THE SURVEY SAYS
2. Which age combination do you think would be most comfortable for you as a mentor? Why?

YOUNGER OR SIMILAR-AGED MENTOR
3. Describe advantages and disadvantages in a mentor being similar in age to her merea.

MENTORING PAIRS 2–20 YEARS APART
4. Describe advantages and disadvantages in a mentor being 2-20 years older than her merea.

MENTORING PAIRS 21–40 YEARS APART
5. Describe advantages and disadvantages in a mentor being 21-40 years older than her merea.

MENTORING PAIRS SEPARATED BY 41 OR MORE YEARS
6. Describe advantages and disadvantages in a mentor being 41 or more years older than her merea.

HOW RUTH AND NAOMI USED AGE DIFFERENCE TO THEIR ADVANTAGE
7. When you unscrambled the words in the exercise "The Blessings of Youth/The Blessings of Age," what unique qualities specific to youth and to age did you identify that blessed Ruth and Naomi's relationship? Can you think of other qualities not listed?

PRAYER NEEDS:
- I want to be open to whatever age combination the Lord provides me and my merea.
- I fear I may not be able to bridge the age gap. I need courage and boldness to believe in myself.
- I want to embrace the characteristics of my own and my merea's age difference.

CHAPTER EIGHTEEN
From Covenant to Closure

SUPPLIES:
Minimum

1. Read aloud "The Potter's Wheel." How do you see yourself on the Potter's wheel as you engage in the mentoring relationship?
2. Read Jeremiah 18:2 together. God said to Jeremiah, "Go down to the potter's house, and there I will give you my message." Have you ever received a message from God as you went to a certain place?

LEAVING A LEGACY
3 Review the meaning of the word *closure*. What does the word *closure* mean to you? Can you think of relationships in which you have experienced closure?

GREATER THINGS YOU WILL DO
4. Describe some of the miraculous deeds Elisha performed after his mentor, Elijah, was gone. In what ways would you like to mentor your merea so well that she exceeds you in spiritual growth and ministry?

THE LAW OF DIMINISHING EXPERTISE
5. Review the meaning of "The Law of Diminishing Expertise." Share an experience in your life that illustrates "The Law of Diminishing Expertise."
6. How do you feel about "working yourself out of a job" as a mentor?

FROM CLOSURE TO COVENANT
7. What is meant by the phrase *From Closure to Covenant*? Have you been in a mentoring relationship to the point of renegotiating the relationship? What happened?

RITES OF PASSAGE
8. What gift(s) did you choose as a rite of passage for the closure phase of your mentor/merea relationship?

PRAYER NEEDS:
• I want to have appropriate closure to this stage of my relationship with my merea.
• I want to have the right spirit as my merea grows and perhaps exceeds me in ministry.
• I need to know the kind of relationship my merea and I should continue.

WOW! YOU DID IT!

Now That You've Completed This Study

Wow! You did it! Here's a high-five for taking risks and following through with this demanding course of study. The Lord will continue to prepare you. Much of your training will occur on the job.

Decide as a group if you would like to continue to meet to share and pray for each other as you mentor. If you decide to meet, decide the date now and plan for your time together. Another idea would be to plan a fellowship event where you could discuss your future plans.

If you have not yet begun mentoring, consider having a commissioning service to recognize and pray for your mentors. We have included a copy of the service for your use.

As you close the last chapter of this study, another chapter begins. You get to write this one. Write lots of loving, patient words to yourself and your merea. Write about the awesome grace of your Savior. Write about your hurts and disappointments to the Lord. He hears you. He loves you because you are a woman after God's own heart.

Love,

Edna and Tricia

HOW TO USE THIS BOOK IN YOUR CHURCH

Among the church women's leaders we surveyed whose mentoring ministries fizzled out, a common cause seemed to be failure to establish bonding relationships between mentors and mereas and between mentors and other mentors in the church. We believe these suggestions will help you complete a successful mentoring ministry to help young mereas in their spiritual walk.

1. Pray about God's will in beginning a Merea Movement in your church. Ask for His wisdom to guide you each step of the way if you feel He is leading you to begin.

2. Poll (formally, with a survey, or informally, in conversation) the young women or the new Christians in your church to see if they feel the need for mentors.

3. Approach spiritually mature women in the church whom you consider potential mentors. Discuss the need for mentors and ask them to pray about serving as mentors in a church ministry. (We have found that reversing steps # 2 and # 3 is ineffective. Most mereas catch a vision for a church Merea Movement first; then when older, more spiritually mature women see the need, they respond affirmatively. They have the spiritual and life-experience resources to offer once they see the need, but they may never begin a mentoring ministry in the church on their own. If you have a vision for this Merea Movement in your church, share it first with mereas and then with mentors.

4. Share the vision with your pastor. Overwhelmingly, pastors have favored Merea Movements in their churches as a tool for outreach and discipleship.

5. Organize a leadership team to pray and plan. Let the Holy Spirit lead as you decide on budget needs, times to meet (weekly, monthly, perhaps a yearly celebration of successes), prayer supporters for the ministry, length of service (usually six months or a year; then renegotiating the terms of each mentoring relationship), church calendar concerns, community concerns, and other concerns you feel led to discuss.

6. Devise a way to find mereas and mentors interested in the ministry in your church. (Remember, a woman may be a mentor but also may want someone more spiritually mature to mentor her; therefore, she can be a merea, too. It's all right to be both merea and mentor.) To find out who wants to participate in this ministry, have some women's leaders give out an interest survey in Sunday School classes and others send out forms in a letter or newsletter to all church members. The survey will ask respondents to list their needs, their gifts, and their interests in general, and will give them a chance to sign up to be a merea or a mentor. Decide if you want to limit the Merea Movement to women, or if you find a need among the men in your church to mentor more spiritually immature men as well.

7. Once you have a list of names of potential mereas and mentors, decide the best way to match them. In a small church, you may know instinctively which personalities will blend well. In a large church, you may need to form a team to look carefully over the surveys of needs and to pray fervently as they match mereas and mentors, trying to get compatible factors in place for each mentoring relationship.

8. Plan a time for the mentors and mereas to meet. This may be done at a breakfast, a luncheon, a banquet, or another meal. It may also be done at a meeting in the church or at a neutral location such as a home or a community center (see suggestions for themes and decorations at the end of this list of suggestions). You may want to plan an overnight prayer retreat with a more elaborate gifts evaluation, such as the Key to Me Seminars listed in the Resources and Recommended Reading page at the back of this book.

9. Plan a commissioning service for mentors (see a sample on page 133). The commissioning may be a part of the introductory meeting, or you may hold it at an alternate time. You may want to ask a guest to speak at this meeting or at your prayer retreat; perhaps someone like Vickie Kraft, Esther Burroughs, Daisy Hepburn, Barbara Joiner, Donna Otto, or another author of a women's book who knows mentoring firsthand.

10. Include in your instructions to mentoring pairs a way for them to take advantage of a "painless back-out" period in which either the merea or the mentor can back out of the relationship with no stigma attached. (In case the relationship doesn't gel from the beginning or there is conflict, everyone who participates should be given options.)

    Also, include instructions for things mereas and mentors can do together (see "Things You Can Do with Your Merea"). Decide if you want to make Bible study mandatory. Most mentoring ministries do make this a must. If a Bible study already exists, your Merea Movement can dovetail with it; if not, you may want to enlist a study leader to teach a weekly Bible study at an appropriate time which suits the mentoring pairs' schedules. Offer options when possible. We suggest the mentors use this book as a Bible study meeting when it's suitable for them. They have special needs for advice and support from other mentors as they encounter real challenges in the mentoring process. They also need each other for encouragement to prevent burnout. (See "What You Need to Know Before You Read This Book" for suggestions on training mentors for the mentoring relationship.)

    Suggest ways mentors and mereas can keep in touch (telephone, notes, email, visits, meals).

11. Suggest ways mentors and mereas can enlist prayer support. This book (chapter 16) suggests each mentor find three women who will pray for her faithfully as she mentors her merea.

12. Suggest ways to follow up. Good follow-up is essential for keeping the mentoring ministry active and for assuring a deep bonding of participants which encourages enthusiasm for future participation.

THEME SUGGESTIONS

GARDENING

This follows the theme of Esther Burroughs's book, *A Garden Path to Mentoring: Planting Your Life in Another and Releasing the Fragrance of Christ*.

One church in Mississippi has used this theme effectively: They based their first year's ministry on Scriptures about gardening. At the fall Merea Movement kickoff, they used aluminum watering cans with graceful spouts as centerpieces for luncheon tables. Watering cans filled with fall flowers and seed packets scattered around the tables finished the scene. Their speaker was Esther Burroughs, who spoke on planting spiritual seed and cultivating our mereas as we would cultivate flowers. As a follow-up to this meeting, they had a commissioning service for each mentor and held a special consecration and prayer meeting for mentoring pairs.

At the winter Merea Movement meeting, each watering can was filled with bare sticks. Moss and bare bulbs decorated serving tables. The speaker brought a message about germination, dormancy, and waiting. In the spring, the watering cans were used again, this time surrounded by blossoming bulbs: hyacinths, daffodils, and tulips. The speaker talked of blossoming relationships and earnest mentoring growth.

The summer meeting was a profuse decoration of lush summer roses in each watering can, surrounded by other signs of summer. The speaker gave suggestions for a continuing, vibrant Merea Movement that reproduces and grows deeper with each day.

With this theme, use gardening tools as favors or prizes; attach name tags to flower corsages; use long-stemmed roses for mentors to present to their mereas during the commissioning service or during the introduction meeting.

OPEN HEARTS AND HOMES

Based on the theme in 1 Peter 4:8–10, you can use dollhouses with furniture, ceramic villages, or gingerbread houses as table decorations. You may offer a cookie exchange, a tasting party, or household hints as added features. Each mentor may present to her merea her recipe for a spiritual banquet to usher her into the presence of the King of Kings.

AAA–ANOINTED, APPOINTED ANGELS

Based on Luke 2:10, Isaiah 61:1, Titus 2, and/or other Scriptures, you may use Christmas angels of all sorts and shapes during the year. You can use angel treetop ornaments all year. Speakers may talk about the words of the angels (*Fear not*), or they may choose to talk about how God anoints us to serve Him as mentors and how He appoints us for special ministries as we guide others in the mentoring adventure.

TEDDY BEAR PICNIC

Decorated picnic baskets filled with teddy bears and food make good centerpieces. Ask mentors and mereas to bring their old teddy bears or write about their childhood teddy bears. Place balloons in the teddy bear hands or give teddy bear favors such as pencils, erasers, or candy. Base your meetings on Philippians 4:11, Proverbs 17:22, Romans 12:13, or 1 John 4:7. (You may choose other toys, such as Raggedy Ann dolls, as a similar theme.)

OTHER

Brainstorm with your leadership team your favorite Scriptures and themes. Have fun as you plan!

THINGS YOU CAN DO WITH YOUR MEREA

- ❑ Participate in a Bible study at church, in another's home, at school, at work, etc.
- ❑ Study the Bible together—just the two of you.
- ❑ Go to church together on Sundays or other days.
- ❑ Go to Christian Women's Club or other Christian activities in your town.
- ❑ Participate together in your church's ministry projects.
- ❑ Join a Christian book club together.
- ❑ Go on local shop-till-you-drop trips with other church women or by yourselves.
- ❑ Take a weekly excursion to the grocery store.
- ❑ Walk in the local malls.
- ❑ Organize and/or join others in group trips out of town to major outlet malls.
- ❑ Pray together for church needs.
- ❑ Pray at a certain time each day wherever you are.
- ❑ Pray for each other's personal or family needs.
- ❑ Join each other for a cup of coffee in the mornings.
- ❑ Join each other for a cup of tea in the afternoons.
- ❑ When your children nap, enjoy quiet time together.
- ❑ When your teenagers go to a prom, chaperone together.
- ❑ Entertain each other's family for dinner.
- ❑ Serve her family; play maid for a day.
- ❑ Write affirmation notes, mail cards, or send flowers for special occasions.
- ❑ Baby-sit for a mom's night out.
- ❑ Jointly baby-sit for someone else who desperately needs a break.
- ❑ Enjoy a sport or exercise together.
- ❑ Learn a new skill together (smocking, knitting, crocheting, or cake decorating).
- ❑ Read the same novels; discuss later.
- ❑ Start a collection together, based on a common interest.
- ❑ Share recipes (specialize in Chinese, Italian, French, Jewish recipes, or others).
- ❑ Share tips on car care.
- ❑ Take a class at a local college or community center.
- ❑ Get your CPR certification together.
- ❑ Visit museums in nearby towns; take a few children with you.
- ❑ Go on a silent retreat at a nearby monastery.
- ❑ Email each other often.
- ❑ Surf the net for each other's interests. Share what you find.
- ❑ Email flowers through the World Wide Web (www): 1800flowers.com.
- ❑ Email cards through the Internet: bluemountain.com.
- ❑ Write a journal of your experiences together.
- ❑ Have a "food swap" for dinner. Each of you cooks more than she needs and shares dishes with the other's family. This works especially well if you live in the same neighborhood and each has to prepare dinner for her family at a similar time.
- ❑ Give each other household hints (e.g., use hair spray to remove ink stains).
- ❑ Serve one day a week together (or once a month, etc.) in the church office.
- ❑ Ride to work or to school together.
- ❑ Carpool each other's children.
- ❑ Do something daring together (hot air balloon ride, rock climbing).
- ❑ Go prayer walking in your neighborhood. Stop and pray when God directs. Pray about certain situations, appearance of homes, people who live there, trouble.
- ❑ Prayer walk in the inner city.
- ❑ Plan a mentoring weekend retreat based on *A Garden Path to Mentoring* by Esther Burroughs (New Hope Publishers).

MENTOR/MEREA COVENANT

*L*ord, thank You for the relationship You have begun.

I, _____ ,

and I _____ ,

enter into this covenant friendship with joy.
As evidence of our commitment to this mentoring
relationship, we each agree to do the following:

- Commit to meeting together regularly.
- Make an effort to prepare for study times together.
- Keep personal information shared within the mentoring relationship private. If a need to consult someone outside the relationship arises, we will discuss it together.
- Strive for honesty and openness in all interactions between mentor and merea.
- Other _____

Mentor

I, _____ ,

accept your call to mentor to your beloved child and

my friend, _____ .

Date _____

Merea

I, _____ ,

accept the invitation to be mentored by Your dear servant and my friend,

_____ .

Date _____

COMMISSIONING SERVICE FOR MENTORS

THE CALL

Call mentor candidates forward and have them face the speaker, backs to the congregation (optional position—face forward).

Speaker: (To congregation) Today we come before God and His people to consecrate and commission these women as mentors. We publicly recognize and affirm God's calling them to this ministry of serving, encouraging, teaching, counseling, and guiding another woman so that she may bring God glory through her life. The woman who is mentored will be called the merea ("mah-RAY-ah"), a Hebrew word for friend, to signify that while she is a disciple and a learner, she must first be loved as a friend.

Speaker: (To mentor candidates) As God commanded Moses to remove his shoes in honor of God's holy presence, please remove your shoes in recognition of God's holy presence and calling on your life. God cares for your merea and is preparing you to minister in her life. The following Scripture is adapted from Exodus, chapters three and four. I will read God's words and you respond in unison, as Moses responded.

Speaker: The LORD says: I have seen your merea's needs. I have heard her cry. I am concerned about her, and I have come to help. I will bring her out of that land and lead her to a good land. So now I am sending you.

Candidates: I am not great, Lord, how can I go?

Speaker: I will be with you. This will be proof that I am sending you: After you lead her out, you both will worship me in this place.

Candidates: But, Lord, I have never been a skilled speaker. I can't find the right words.

Speaker: Who made your voice? It is I, the LORD.

Now go. I will help you speak, and I will teach you what to say.

THE COMMITMENT

Speaker: Jesus showed us how to minister with the attitude and humility of a servant. At His last meal with His disciples He took a towel and a bowl of water and kneeled to wash His disciples' feet. He then asked, "Do you understand what I have done for you? If I, your Lord and Teacher, have washed your feet, you also should wash each other's feet." (John 13:13–14 NCV)

(To candidates): Please kneel (or be seated) in recognition of your role as a servant. Please respond to the following statements by speaking in unison.

Speaker: As a mentor who serves, God invites you to use your spiritual gifts, talents, and skills to bless your merea.

Candidates: Even so, Lord, send me.

Speaker: As Deborah encouraged Barak and instilled in him the confidence to face battle, so will your merea need your encouragement and belief in her.

Candidates: Even so, Lord, send me.

Speaker: As a mentor who teaches another, Christ urges you to apply yourself to grow in knowledge and understanding of His ways. Let His truth live in you and from that life teach your merea.

Candidates: Even so, Lord, send me.

Speaker: Isaiah says Christ gathers the lambs in His arms and carries them close to His heart. As you carry your merea close to your heart, you will also carry her burdens. As you share her load, she will look to you for wisdom and nurture. Listen intently; advise carefully; pray fervently. Walk beside her always.

Candidates: *Even so, Lord, send me.*

Speaker: Your merea will be watching you. She does not need to see perfection. She will need to see that you are human—that your wish is not to mold a person after your own likeness, but rather to mirror the love of the Savior.

Candidates: *Even so, Lord, send me.*

The Consecration

Speaker: (To congregation and candidates) Let us pray.

(*Speaker leads in prayer*): Lord, your servant hears your call, makes the commitment, and accepts your commission to serve as a mentor. Guard her home and her heart. Keep her motives and her life pure. Empower her to live honestly and faithfully as she lays down her life as a mentor for her merea—her friend.

Presentation of Candidates

Speaker: (To candidates) Please stand and face the congregation. (Ask congregation to stand as well.)

(Present candidates to the congregation) The Lord says, "Here is my servant, whom I uphold, my chosen one in whom I delight." (Isaiah 42:1 KJV)

Speaker: (To congregation) Please repeat after me the following phrases from the Scriptures to express your support in prayer and encouragement to these ladies:

Sing, O daughter;
Be glad and rejoice with all your heart.
The Lord your God takes great delight in you.
He comforts you with His love.
He rejoices over you with singing.
(paraphrased, Zeph. 3:14–17 NIV)

Mentors (Respond in unison): **Behold the handmaid of the Lord; be it unto me according to thy word.** (Luke 1:38 KJV)

CONSECRATION OF MEREAS (OPTIONAL)

If mereas are known and in the congregation, they may be asked to come forward for consecration at this time. The mereas may kneel while mentors lay hands on them (or stand holding hands with their mentors).

Speaker: Mentors, please repeat after me the following prayer for your merea:
    This is my prayer for you, that your love will grow more and more;
    that you will have knowledge and understanding with your love;
    that you will see the difference between good and bad and will choose the good;
    that you will be pure and without wrong for the coming of Christ;
    that you will do many good things with the help of Christ to bring glory and praise to God.

    (Philippians 1:9–11 NCV)

Close the service with the song, **"Make Me a Servant,"** or another appropriate hymn.

RESOURCES AND READINGS

William Backus, *Telling Each Other the Truth* (Minneapolis: Bethany House, 1985).

Esther Burroughs, *A Garden Path to Mentoring: Planting Your Life in Another and Releasing the Fragrance of Christ* (Birmingham: New Hope Publishers, 1997).

Stuart Calvert, *Uniquely Gifted* (Birmingham: New Hope Publishers, 1993).

Sue Carver, *A Key to Me Seminars*, 4647 T Highway 280, Suite 271, Birmingham, AL 35242. Email:kahlercsc@aol.com (this is an on-site seminar for mentors available for your church or organization.) Includes a 40-page booklet on each individual; learning principles of communicating; sharing in exercises demonstrating different styles, applying concepts learned, and developing a strategy for reducing distress. Seminars range from half a day to three days in length.

Linda Clark, compiler, *5 Leadership Essentials for Women* (Birmingham: New Hope Publishers, 2004).

Dr. Henry Cloud and Dr. John Townsend, *Boundaries* (Grand Rapids: Zondervan, 1992).

John W. Drakeford, and Claude King, *Wise Counsel: Skills for Lay Counseling* (Nashville: The Sunday School Board of the Southern Baptist Convention, 1988).

Ted Engstrom with Norman B. Rohrer, *The Fine Art of Mentoring* (Newburgh, Ind.: Trinity Press, 1989).

Charlene J. Gray, compiler, Trudy Johnson, ed., *No Longer Forgotten: The Remarkable Story of Christian Women's Job Corps* (Birmingham: New Hope Publishers, 1998).

Brenda Hunter, *In the Company of Women: Deepening Our Relationships with the Important Women in Our Lives* (Sisters: OR: Questar Publishers, 1995).

Barbara Joiner, *Yours for the Giving* (Birmingham: New Hope Publishers, 2004).

Vickie Kraft, *Women Mentoring Women: Ways to Start, Maintain, and Expand a Biblical Women's Ministry* (Chicago: Moody Press, 1992).

Robert S. McGee, *The Search for Significance* (Houston, TX.: Rapha Publishing, 1990).

Donna Otto, *Between Women of God* (Eugene, Ore.: Harvest House Publishers, 1995).

Donna Otto, *Mentors for Mothers: Passing on the Convictions of Our Hearts, the Passions of Our Lives* (Scottsdale, Ariz.: D & D Publishers, 1997).

Carol Porter and Mike Hamel, eds., *Women's Ministry Handbook* (USA: Victor Books, 1992).

Gail Sheehy, *New Passages: Mapping Your Life Across Time* (New York: Ballantine Books, 1995).

Richard Swenson, *Margin: Restoring Emotional, Physical, Financial and Time Reserves to Overloaded Lives* (Colorado Springs: NAVpress, 1992).

Charles Swindoll, *Improving Your Serve* (Waco: Word Inc., 1981).

Warren Wiersbe, *Be Real* (Wheaton: Victor Books, 1972).

Also by Edna Ellison

Friend to Friend: *Enriching Friendships Through a Shared Study of Philippians*
Ideal for two women to experience together, this study is written to enrich friendships between women as they grow in Christ.
1-56309-710-9

Friendships of Faith:
A Shared Study of Hebrews
Second in the Friend to Friend series, designed for two friends to experience together, *Friendships of Faith* is a straightforward study of the most basic tenets of the Christian faith as outlined in the book of Hebrews.
1-56309-762-1

Friendships of Purpose:
A Shared Study of Ephesians
Third in the Friend to Friend series, designed for two friends to experience together, *Friendships of Purpose* is written for those seeking growth and fellowship within the Christian family.
1-56309-901-2

Available in Christian bookstores everywhere.

new
hope
PUBLISHERS

Inspiring Women. Changing Lives.